Case Scenarios in Hospitality Supervision

Join us on the web at

www.hospitality-tourism.delmar.com

Case Scenarios in Hospitality Supervision

Peter Szende

DELMAR
CENGAGE Learning™

Australia • Brazil • Japan • Korea • Mexico • Singapore • Spain • United Kingdom • United States

Case Scenarios in Hospitality Supervision
Peter Szende

Vice President, Career and Professional
  Editorial: Dave Garza

Director of Learning Solutions: Sandy Clark

Senior Acquisitions Editor: James Gish

Managing Editor: Larry Main

Product Manager: Anne Orgren

Editorial Assistant: Sarah Timm

Vice President, Career and Professional
  Marketing: Jennifer McAvey

Marketing Director: Wendy Mapstone

Senior Marketing Manager: Kristin McNary

Marketing Coordinator: Scott Chrysler

Production Director: Wendy Troeger

Senior Content Project Manager:
  Glenn Castle

Art Director: Bethany Kirchmayer

Technology Project Manager:
  Jamilynne Myers

For product information and technology assistance, contact us at
Cengage Learning Customer & Sales Support, 1-800-354-9706
For permission to use material from this text or product, submit all requests online at **www.cengage.com/permissions.**
Further permissions questions can be e-mailed to
permissionrequest@cengage.com

Library of Congress Control Number: 2009924302

ISBN-13: 978-1-4283-2140-3
ISBN-10: 1-4283-2140-3

Delmar
5 Maxwell Drive
Clifton Park, NY 12065-2919
USA

Cengage Learning is a leading provider of customized learning solutions with office locations around the globe, including Singapore, the United Kingdom, Australia, Mexico, Brazil, and Japan. Locate your local office at:
international.cengage.com/region

Cengage Learning products are represented in Canada by Nelson Education, Ltd.

To learn more about Delmar, visit **www.cengage.com/delmar**

Purchase any of our products at your local college store or at our preferred online store **www.ichapters.com**

Notice to the Reader
Publisher does not warrant or guarantee any of the products described herein or perform any independent analysis in connection with any of the product information contained herein. Publisher does not assume, and expressly disclaims, any obligation to obtain and include information other than that provided to it by the manufacturer. The reader is expressly warned to consider and adopt all safety precautions that might be indicated by the activities described herein and to avoid all potential hazards. By following the instructions contained herein, the reader willingly assumes all risks in connection with such instructions. The publisher makes no representations or warranties of any kind, including but not limited to, the warranties of fitness for particular purpose or merchantability, nor are any such representations implied with respect to the material set forth herein, and the publisher takes no responsibility with respect to such material. The publisher shall not be liable for any special, consequential, or exemplary damages resulting, in whole or part, from the readers' use of, or reliance upon, this material.

Printed in the United States of America
1 2 3 4 5 6 7 XXX 12 11 10 09

Contents

Part 8   Relationship with Your Boss   157

Part 9   Managing a Diverse Workforce   173

Threshold: he case method is proving itself to be a very effective tool in hospitality programs. Case studies give students the opportunity to develop problem-solving skills and to think critically. They will allow students to explore contrary points of view relative to a variety of questions.

This collection of case vignettes present scenarios, most requiring management decisions and/or actions. Although most of the cases are very short, they are challenging without being overwhelming. Many of these cases are based on actual business situations I personally encountered throughout my hospitality career. Over the last six years, I have used many of these cases in teaching and tested their relevance with students.

The seventy-five vignettes are organized into nine sections that reflect human resources–related challenges that are pertinent for hospitality managers. A correlation table shows the connection between vignettes and covered subjects. Topics include many of the issues a supervisor is confronted with on a daily basis. The skills and competencies necessary to deal with these problems are discussed throughout this book.

The vignettes may be used to stimulate class discussion or introduce students to HR management topics. Each case concludes with a list of questions for the student to answer concerning the scenarios they are given. The instructor's manual provides a comprehensive analysis of the cases, suggested answers and solutions to questions, and alternative approaches for presenting the materials.

This book can complement any hospitality management curriculum (including Human Resources Management, Supervision, Leadership, and Organizational Behavior) and will reinforce theories and concepts that students study throughout the course.

Supplements

Electronic Access Codes

The electronic access codes provided with this text allow students to read the case studies on-line, and to submit responses to the discussion questions electronically via WebCT, Blackboard, or Angel. The codes also provide access to an on-line discussion forum.

Instructor's Manual

This text is accompanied by a robust instructor's manual containing detailed exploration of each case and suggestions for guiding student discussions.

Acknowledgements

I would like to thank Treci Bonime, Sam Everett, and Lynda Hebach who offered valuable feedback. Their comments were pivotal in the development of the text.

The author and publisher would like to thank the following reviewers:

Paul William Howe
Herkimer County Community College
Herkimer, NY

Carl J. Pfaffenberg
Stephen F. Austin State University
Nacogdoches, TX

Peter Ricci
Florida Atlantic University
Boca Raton, FL

Anthony Strianese
Schenectady County Community College
Schenectady, NY

Introduction

The book is structured using specific case presentation styles. A variety of case types exist that differ according to format and/or intended learning outcomes (Lundberg, Rainsford, Shay, & Young, 2001). Thus, these cases are written in a variety of presentation styles. This range in case presentation makes the cases more appealing for the students and illustrates that the daily challenges of hotel life can be reflected in a number of forms.

The five class presentation styles used are as follows:

1. Incident Cases

The case often describes a single incident in somewhat specific detail, circumscribed by time and place. The student's task is to compare the incident with either generally accepted practices and/or his or her own experience. Issues of problem identification are addressed. Students may be asked to determine what additional information is necessary or helpful and to surmise how the organizational context of the incident would impact the situation.

2. Head Cases

In this type of case, one or more principal actors' interactions, activities, thoughts, and feelings are described. The student's task is to surface the assumptions, reasoning, attitudes, or needs to basically get inside the principal's head and see how these are manifested in patterned action and interaction.

3. Application Cases

This type of case describes the application of a management technique or describes a situation in which the student can apply some known technique. Such cases typically provide much information, but it may be highly unstructured. The student's task is to state how the manager performs the task and what the manager must take into account to be more effective.

4. Data Cases

The student's usual task is to find ideas in descriptions and/or to organize these data in some meaningful way. By doing this, students also learn to better consumers of information.

5. Issue Cases

In an issue case, a matter or point is in question (e.g., is the manager's behavior appropriate?). The student's task is to understand and appreciate the antecedents, contexts, and dynamics of the salient issue.

JOURNAL OF MANAGEMENT EDUCATION (1991-) by Craig C. Lundsberg, Peter Rainsford, Jeff P. Shay, Cheri A. Young. Copyright 2001 by Sage Publications Inc. Journals. Reproduced with permission of Sage Publications Inc. Journals in the format Textbook via Copyright Clearance Center.

(This above classification is not exclusive; many of the cases embrace the characteristics of more than one case type.)

Reference

Lundberg, C. C., Rainsford, P., Shay, J. P., & Young, C. A. (2001). Case writing reconsidered. *Journal of Management Education, 25*(4), 450–463.

Matrix of Cases & Subjects

The case presentation styles are listed across the top of the chart. The numbers represent the vignette. For instance, Accepting Criticism is considered a Head Case and can be found at vignette number 62.

MAIN SUBJECTS	INCIDENT CASE	HEAD CASE	APPLICATION CASE	DATA CASE	ISSUE CASE
Accepting Criticism		62			
ADA	23	9	3		
Analytical					41
Anger			17, 46		
Assertiveness	14	54, 62	17, 18		16
Authority	14, 37, 48, 50, 51, 55, 56	1, 21, 49, 53, 54, 61	19		13, 40, 52, 58, 59
Bias			64		
Big picture		57			13, 16, 41, 42
Bullying					39
Buy-in	48		17, 19		12, 16
Chain of command		1, 21, 61			39, 52, 58, 59
Change	55		17, 19		12, 16, 38
Coaching	14, 23	33, 47, 61, 67	19, 25, 45, 46		22, 26, 32, 34, 38, 39, 40, 41, 42, 43, 72
Controlling costs	48			8, 31	16
Credibility	55, 56	54, 61	19		12, 52, 58
Decision making			19		16, 34
Delegation		57			13
Defensiveness	55	47, 54, 62	18		
Discrimination	20	5, 6, 65, 66, 67, 68	3, 64	4	63, 72, 75
Discipline	48, 50, 51, 55, 74	47, 49, 53, 54	45, 46		
Diversity	20, 71, 74	5, 65, 66, 67, 68, 70	3, 64	4	63, 72, 73, 75
Feedback	14, 36	21, 33, 35, 47, 61, 62, 70	18, 25, 30, 46		32, 34, 38, 39, 41
Flexibility	48	9			13, 43
Gossip	36, 56				
Harassment	15, 69, 71	11, 70			39
Hands-on		57			13
Humor/sarcasm	15	35			

(continues)

Continued (from previous page)

MAIN SUBJECTS	INCIDENT CASE	HEAD CASE	APPLICATION CASE	DATA CASE	ISSUE CASE
Incivility	14	35			39
Influence	14	60	19		12, 13, 59
Insubordination	48, 50, 51, 74	53, 54			
Job design/ Job description	50, 74	1, 9			24, 29
Leadership styles			19		
Managing up	56	57, 61, 62			58, 59
Micro-management		57			
Meetings	14	35			38
Motivation		27, 60	30	31	26, 28, 29
Open-door policy		11, 53, 61			52, 58
Organizational politics	37, 56	60, 61	30		58
Organizational structure	14, 37	1			28, 44, 52
Perfectionism		57			42
Performance appraisal	20	21	25		39
Prejudice			64		
Productivity	48	9		8	22, 24
Promotion		60			28, 72
Rapport	14	33, 47	17, 18		
Recruiting/ selection	37	5, 6, 10, 65	2, 3, 7	4	
Religion	20				73
Respect	55	35, 54, 70	30		16
Rewards		27		31	26, 28
Self-confidence		10, 21, 33			13, 32, 39, 40
Stereotypes		70	64		75
Unpopular decisions			17		12, 16
Team building	37		17		44
Trust	55	11, 57	19		16, 32, 52
Workaholism					43
Work systems					24, 26, 44

The Royal Hotel

To make the cases more accessible and to keep them consistent, all scenarios unfold in the same fictitious hotel. The organization chart of the Royal Hotel will provide students with the names and job titles of the main characters. Many of the characters are lower level supervisors, exactly the type of roles most of our students expect to assume shortly after graduation. This will add to the real-life feeling and will help students to bridge the gap between classroom and industry.

ROYAL HOTEL

Overlooking the scenic Bedford River, the Royal Hotel is in the center of the city and just a short drive from the airport. Built a century ago, this landmark hotel features a stone façade flanked by two golden lions. The Royal Hotel radiates Victorian splendor less than two blocks from shopping on Commercial Street. The grandeur of the Royal Hotel coupled with its reputation for impeccable service promises a truly memorable experience.

The Royal's lobby retains many original features and is warmed by an open fireplace. The 400 guest rooms feature views of either Bedford River or the City Park. Separate seating areas offer comfortable reading chairs and Italian leather desks. Bathrooms feature marble countertops and floors, terrycloth bathrobes, and complimentary toiletries. The hotel's health club features an indoor lap pool with palm trees, a fitness room, saunas, and treatment rooms. The hotel maintains its Victorian ambiance with intimate meeting rooms and a spectacular ballroom showcasing antique mahogany furnishings, oil paintings, and wood paneling. The Harvest Room restaurant offers an extensive à la carte menu comprised of international selections and regional favorites. The Riverside Lounge and Bar serves light meals and cocktails and offers a specialty martini menu. Room service is available 24-hours a day.

The Royal hotel is currently a nonunionized environment.

The Royal Hotel's Organizational Chart

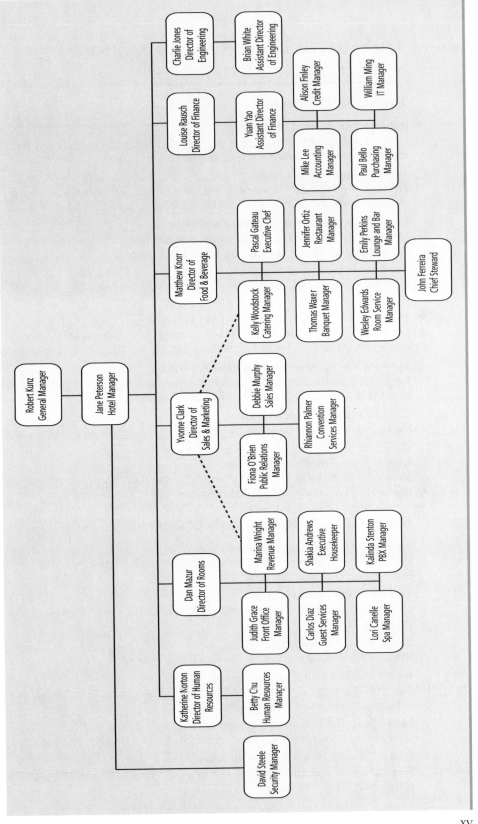

The Royal Hotel's Organizational Structure [Key Positions]

The Executive Committee

Robert Kunz, General Manager
Directs hotel operations by developing and implementing strategies and services that meet or exceed the needs of owners, employees, and guests.

Jane Peterson, Hotel Manager
Oversees the day-to-day operations and assignments of the hotel staff; assists the general manager in the development and communication of departmental strategies and goals.

Katherine Norton, Director of Human Resources
Develops HR strategies, directs all areas of Human Resource administration within the hotel, including employment, salary administration, benefits, and training.

Dan Mazur, Director of Rooms
Provides guidance and leadership to the Rooms division; ensuring consistent compliance of hotel policies; maximizing department profits.

Yvonne Clark, Director of Sales and Marketing
Leads the development and execution of strategic sales and marketing plans and is responsible for developing initiatives in order to achieve budget and revenue goals.

Matthew Knorr, Director of Food and Beverage
Responsible for the overall operation of the Food and Beverage division, ensuring revenues are met and high standards are upheld, and mentoring the F&B managers.

Louise Rausch, Director of Finance
Supervises and directs the financial activities of the hotel, safeguards the assets, and prepares all financial reports.

Charlie Jones, Director of Engineering
Maintains the entire hotel facility, including physical building structure, all mechanical, electrical, HVAC systems, and related equipment.

MANAGERS (Listed in alphabetical order)

Shakia Andrews, Executive Housekeeper
Provides supervision and direction for all housekeeping activities of the hotel; ensures the highest level of cleanliness.

Paul Bello, Purchasing Manager
Oversees the purchasing function of the hotel including food, beverage, and property operation supplies.

Lori Canelle, Spa Manager
Responsible for all aspects of the Health Club operation.

Betty Chu, Human Resources Manager
Assists in the day-to-day management of Human Resources, including recruiting, benefits, employee relations, and training.

Carlos Diaz, Guest Services Manager
Oversees the door attendants, valet parkers, bell staff, gift shop, and concierge employees.

Wesley Edwards, Room Service Manager
Responsible for managing the food and beverage service of in-room dining; ensures that private bars are replenished.

John Ferreira, Chief Steward
Responsible for the set ups of china, glassware, and silverware items for all banquet functions; ensures that the kitchen and back-of-the-house area is clean.

Finely, Credit Manager
Responsible for ensuring that all outstanding balances due to the hotel are paid on a timely basis.

Pascal Gateau, Executive Chef
Responsible for all menu planning, preparation, production, and control for all F&B outlets and banquet facilities.

Judith Grace, Front Office Manager
Oversees all Front Desk operations including guest registrations and checkouts.

Mike Lee, Accounting Manager
Oversees the hotel's Day Audit, Accounts Payable, Accounts Receivable, and Payroll functions.

William Ming, IT Manager
Responsible for the overall operation of the information technology infrastructure.

Debbie Murphy, Sales Manager
Directs the day-to-day activities of the sales team; promotes group and individual hotel business.

O'Brian, Public Relations Manager
Develops and implements innovative public relations strategies to support the hotel's objectives.

Jennifer Ortiz, Restaurant Manager (The Harvest Room)
Responsible for the daily operations of the restaurant; ensures that staff provides quality service.

Rhiannon Palmer, Convention Services Manager
Coordinates all details pertaining to groups; serves as the primary liaison between groups and hotel departments.

Emily Perkins, Lounge and Bar Manager (The Riverside)
Responsible for the daily operations of the lounge and bar; ensures that staff provides quality service.

David Steele, Security Manager
Supervises the activities of the security staff. Responsibilities include incident reporting, safety inspections, and loss prevention inspections. The security manager reports directly to the hotel manager.

Kalinda Stenton, PBX Manager
Oversees the communications center of the hotel; connects incoming calls; takes messages; executes wake-up calls.

Thomas Waxer, Banquet Manager
Ensures the proper execution of all banquet functions.

Brain White, Assistant Director of Engineering
Runs the day-to-day, routine operations of Engineering.

Marina Wright, Revenue Manager
Responsible for maximizing rooms' revenue through management of the hotel's room inventory and for supervising the day-to-day activities of the Reservations department. The revenue manager reports to the director of Rooms, but works closely with the director of Sales and Marketing.

Kelly Woodstock, Catering Manager
Responsible for the sales and planning of all catered functions. The catering manager reports to the director of Food and Beverage, but works closely with the director of Sales and Marketing.

Yuan Yao, Assistant Director of Finance
Assists with the day-to-day accounting office operation; supports the director of Finance.

Dealing with Employee Problems and Problem Employees—A General Guideline

Everybody has a bad day once in a while. Problems are normal, natural, and human. An employee becomes a problem, when the problem persists, and a pattern is developing. Difficult employees come in varying degrees. Dealing with people simply means dealing with difficult behaviors.

In a large number of cases presented in this book, supervisors will encounter difficult behaviors. According to the references reviewed for this work, here is a general guideline to deal successfully with employee behavior related problems.

1. **Identify The Problem Behavior**

   - State the unsatisfactory behavior in factual terms.
   - What is it about the person's behavior that has an adverse impact on the work being completed?
   - Who is affected by the behavior, and how frequently does it occur?

2. **Recognize The Reasons For The Problem**

   - Acknowledge any underlying causes for the problem behavior.
   - Clues to possible causes of problem behavior can be identified by examining how the employee interacts with others.

3. **Discuss The Behavior With The Employees**

   Engage the person in a private discussion that follows these steps:

   a. State the meeting's purpose.
   b. Describe the behavior's negative impact. Carefully separate the behavior from the person.
   (It's the behavior you object to, not the person.)
   c. Clarify the expectations; model the behavior you want to see.
   d. Explore solutions acceptable to both parties.
   e. Agree on a solution; obtain a commitment on specific actions the person will take.
   f. Set deadlines and progress review dates.

4. **Acknowledge Improved Behavior**

   - Follow up with the person.
   - Recognize and comment on any progress you've observed.
   - Re-evaluate the action plan and revise it as necessary.

Meeting Human Resources Requirements

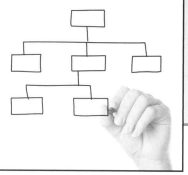

The Organizational Chart

Case Type:	Head Case
Main Subjects:	Authority, Chain of Command, Job Design/ Job Description, Organizational Structure
Who's Who:	• Yvonne Clark, *Director of Sales and Marketing*
	• Matthew Knorr, *Director of Food and Beverage*
	• Robert Kunz, *General Manager*
	• Dan Mazur, *Director of Rooms*
	• Kelly Woodstock, *Catering Manager*
	• Marina Wright, *Revenue Manager*

This morning, the general manager presented the new organizational chart of the Royal Hotel. (See Exhibit A on page xv.) "This chart depicts the hierarchical relationships among divisions, departments, and positions within the Royal Hotel," explained Kunz. "We have a pretty simple structure with direct vertical lines between the different levels of the organization. As you all know, Yvonne is responsible for developing initiatives in order to achieve our budget and revenue goals. As of today, Yvonne will support Marina and Kelly by providing them with her specialized expertise."

Executive committee members looked excited, only Dan and Matthew looked somewhat puzzled.

1. Describe potential conflicts that may arise in line-staff relationships.
   a. From the viewpoint of Yvonne
   b. From the viewpoint of Dan and Matthew
   c. From the viewpoint of Marina and Kelly
2. How can the Royal Hotel minimize the risk of potential conflicts?
3. Identify managers at the Royal Hotel with functional authority.

EXHIBIT 1.1

Royal Hotel—Manager's handbook (excerpts)

THE ROYAL HOTEL ORGANIZATIONAL CHART

At the Royal Hotel, three types of authority are present: line, staff, and functional.

1. The solid lines, referred to as **line authority,** indicate the direct authority a manager has over a subordinate. Line authority flows down the chain of command.

2. **Staff authority** is the right to advise or counsel other subordinates outside of a manager's direct line authority. This reporting relationship is depicted by dotted lines.

3. **Functional authority** covers specific task areas only. It is given to managers who, in order to meet responsibilities in their own areas, must be able to exercise some control over organizational members in other areas.

Notes and Responses to Case Questions:

Red Flags

Case Type:	**Application Case**
Main Subject:	**Recruiting/Selection**
Who's Who:	• Betty Chu, *Human Resources Manager*
	• Judith Grace, *Front Office Manager*
	• Dan Mazur, *Director of Rooms*

Betty from Human Resources (HR) left a voice mail for Dan. "Hi Dan. I understand that Judith is going back to school soon, and you might be looking for another Front Office manager. I e-mailed three applications to you. Just to let you know, I did not have a chance to look for red flags. I have some time next week and would like start with one interview. Could you let me know which one of the three candidates should be called in?"

1. Warning signs/red flags. Often, evidence indicating a bad apple is right on the application or the résumé. Review the applications on the following pages for any items that don't make sense or leave you with an uneasy feeling.

2. Why do some managers believe that long-term, stable applicants may become bad hires?

3. For employers, fake education credentials pose significant problems. Please explain why.

4. What can employers do to prevent candidates from exaggerating or lying about their qualifications or inflating their job titles, job descriptions, or salary histories?

5. Why do you think asking for a salary history can be helpful to HR professionals?

6. Careful reference checking is the best way to objectively evaluate an individual's job performance over time and from different point of view. Suggest questions to ask about candidates who have changed jobs frequently.

Attachment: Three Application Forms

Application Form 1

THE ROYAL HOTEL
ℛ

Employment Application

Applicant Information				
Full Name:	SMITH	MARY	W.	Date: 1/3/2009
	Last	*First*	*M.I.*	

Education

College:	BALTIMORE COLLEGE	Major:	HOSPITALITY		
From: 2002	To: 2006	Did you graduate?	YES ☑ NO ☐	Degree:	B.S.
Other:		Major:			
From:	To:	Did you graduate?	YES ☐ NO ☐	Degree:	

Previous Employment

Company:	HOTEL EMPIRE, BALTIMORE	Phone:	(410) 111 - 1111
Job Title:	ASSISTANT FRONT OFFICE MANAGER	Starting Salary: $32,000	Ending Salary: $32,000
Responsibilities:	MAXIMIZED FINANCIAL PERFORMANCE OF HOTEL		
From: 9/1/2008 To: 12/10/2008	Reason for Leaving:	MY DREAM IS TO JOIN THE ROYAL HOTEL	
Company:	HOTEL VICTORIA, BALTIMORE	Phone:	(410) 222 - 2222
Job Title:	FRONT OFFICE SUPERVISOR	Starting Salary: $28,000	Ending Salary: $28,000
Responsibilities:	MANAGED ALL ASPECTS OF THE OPERATION		
From: 4/1/2008 To: 8/15/2008	Reason for Leaving:	OPPORTUNITY TO ASSIST THE OPENING OF HOTEL EMPIRE	
Company:	HOTEL PARK, PHILADELPHIA	Phone:	(215) 333 - 3333
Job Title:	FRONT DESK AGENT	Starting Salary: $10/hour	Ending Salary: $11/HOUR
Responsibilities:	CHECKED GUESTS IN AND OUT OF THE HOTEL		
From: 2007 To: 3/10/2008	Reason for Leaving:	PERSONAL	

References

MR. LOUIS HERMAN, RESTAURANT MANAGER - HOTEL VICTORIA BALTIMORE

MS. ANGELICA BOLD, EXECUTIVE HOUSEKEEPER - HOTEL PARK PHILADELPHIA

Interests/Special Skills/ Clubs

Please list any interests, special skills, clubs or organization to which you belong which directly relate to the job for which you are applying

SKIING, SWIMMING, INLINE SKATING

Application Form 2

THE ROYAL HOTEL

Employment Application

Applicant Information				
Full Name:	Brown	John	B	Date: 1/3/2009
	Last	First	M.I.	

Education						
College:	New Orleans University	Major:	Anthropology			
From: 2001	To: 2005	Did you graduate?	YES ☑	NO ☐	Degree:	B.S.
Other:	New Orleans City College	Major:	Geography			
From: 1999	To: 2001	Did you graduate?	YES ☑	NO ☐	Degree:	Associate Degree

Previous Employment			
Company: Hotel Astoria, New Orleans		Phone:	(504) 555-5555
Job Title: Assistant Front Office Manager	Starting Salary: $33,000	Ending Salary:	$34,000
Responsibilities: Assisted the Front Office Manager in overseeing PBX, concierge and Front Desk. Maintained High quality of standards			
From: 2/1/2008 To: 12/15/2008	Reason for Leaving:	No opportunity for promotion at Hotel Astoria	
Company: Hotel Astoria, New Orleans		Phone:	(504) 555-5555
Job Title: Front Desk Supervisor	Starting Salary: $29,000	Ending Salary:	$29,500
Responsibilities: Supervised Front Desk Staff, Resolved guest concerns			
From: 2/10/2007 To: 1/31/2008	Reason for Leaving: —		
Company: Hotel Astoria, New Orleans		Phone:	(504) 555-5555
Job Title: Front Desk Agent	Starting Salary: $10.50/hour	Ending Salary:	$10.50/hour
Responsibilities: Performed a variety of duties including guest registration and handling of guest inquiries			
From: 6/30/2006 To: 2/9/2007	Reason for Leaving: —		

References
Mr Bruce Gates, Director of Rooms, Hotel Astoria, New Orleans
Mrs Esther LaValle, Human Resources Manager, Hotel Astoria
New Orleans

Interests/Special Skills/ Clubs
Please list any interests, special skills, clubs or organization to which you belong which directly relate to the job for which you are applying
Golf lover, Attends most PGA tournaments

Application Form 3

THE ROYAL HOTEL

Employment Application

Applicant Information

Full Name:	Rogers	Leslie	K	Date:	1/3/2009
	Last	*First*	*M.I.*		

Education

College:	Bellevue University		Major:	Business Administration		
From:	2007	To: 2008	Did you graduate?	YES ☒ NO ☐	Degree:	Ph.D.
Other:	Seattle University		Major:	Hospitality		
From:	2003	To: 2007	Did you graduate?	YES ☒ NO ☐	Degree:	B.S.

Previous Employment

Company:	Hotel Pacific, Seattle		Phone:	(206) 444-4444
Job Title:	Assistant Housekeeper	Starting Salary: $36,000	Ending Salary: $37,000	
Responsibilities:	• Managed day-to-day activities of the department • Scheduled employees to ensure proper coverage			
From: 7/1/2008	To: 12/10/2008	Reason for Leaving:	—	

Company:	Hotel Pacific, Seattle		Phone:	(206) 444-4444
Job Title:	Assistant Front Office Manager	Starting Salary: $30,000	Ending Salary: $31,000	
Responsibilities:	Effectively managed the daily operations of the front desk			
From: 5/4/2003	To: 6/30/2007	Reason for Leaving:		

Company:	The Mansion, Portland		Phone:	(503) 999-9999
Job Title:	Assistant Front Office Manager	Starting Salary: $30,000	Ending Salary: $30,000	
Responsibilities:	Established and maintained attentive and courteous hospitality			
From: 3/7/2001	To: 11/30/2002	Reason for Leaving:	Disagreed with policies	

References

Mr. Greg Ebeliv - Front office Manager - Hotel Pacific, Seattle

Ms. Kate Williams - Executive Housekeeper - Hotel Pacific, Seattle

Interests/Special Skills/ Clubs

Please list any interests, special skills, clubs or organization to which you belong which directly relate to the job for which you are applying

Hiking, Surfing, playing piano and guitar with other musicians.

Notes and Responses to Case Questions:

Candidate Screening

Case Type:	**Application Case**
Main Subject:	**ADA, Discrimination, Diversity, Recruiting/Selection**
Who's Who:	• Shakia Andrews, *Executive Housekeeper*
	• Betty Chu, *Human Resources Manager*

The phone was ringing when Shakia entered her office. It was Betty from HR. "I hope you like it here at the Royal. I look forward to seeing you at the second orientation day next Tuesday." Betty told Shakia. Shakia did not have a chance to answer as Betty continued by saying. "By the way, I've just received another application for the assistant manager position. Would you mind meeting with this individual?"

"Absolutely, I'm available to see the candidate tomorrow, first thing in the morning," Shakia answered.

The next morning, the following conversation occurred between the candidate and the executive housekeeper.

SHAKIA: So, what brings you to the Royal?
CANDIDATE: I have heard so many great things about this hotel.

SHAKIA: (glances at the application) Do you wish to be addressed as Mrs.? Ms? or Miss?
CANDIDATE: It really doesn't matter; feel free to call me Mary.

SHAKIA: (still looking at the application form) What is your maiden name?
CANDIDATE: My name is Mary Kispesti.

SHAKIA: You have a very unusual last name. What is its origin?
CANDIDATE: (laughing) I am not sure. I know more about the origin of my first name.

SHAKIA: (trying to put the candidate at ease) What a gloomy day. It's almost 8 A.M. but still so dark. Nice dress, Mary. Is it matching the color of your eyes?
CANDIDATE: (thinking) I am not sure. At home everybody says that I have greenish-hazel eyes.

SHAKIA: (laughing) Are you sure about that? For me they look brownish. What language is spoken at home?
CANDIDATE: Mostly English.

SHAKIA: Where do you see yourself in five years?

CANDIDATE: (becomes talkative) As you can see in my resume I have gained tremendous experience in the hotel industry and I would really like to work my way up to become a department head. I know very well that your hotel has very high standards and I really would like to live up your expectations on a long-term basis. I am a responsible woman and would be interested in what your thoughts are on career versus marriage.

SHAKIA: (hesitating) Mary, I am not married.

SHAKIA: (after a brief pause) You know, it's a physically demanding job. Do you have any disability that would prevent you from performing the job?

CANDIDATE: No, I can do this job.

SHAKIA: Reliability is a key requirement at the Royal. How many days were you absent from work last year because of illness?

CANDIDATE: Two or three.

SHAKIA: Mary, we need someone who is fully flexible. Can you work during major holidays like Christmas?

CANDIDATE: Sure, I am available any time.

SHAKIA: How about on Saturdays and Sundays?

CANDIDATE: No problem.

SHAKIA: As you know, at this point we are only screening applicants. However, I may need to quickly get in contact with you. What is the name and address of the relative to be notified in case of an emergency?

CANDIDATE: I can give you the name of a cousin.

SHAKIA: Alright Mary, we'll be in touch. Let me walk with you to your car.

CANDIDATE: Actually I took public transportation.

1. Outline the problems with this interview.
2. What advice might you give to the Royal Hotel?

Notes and Responses to Case Questions:

C a s e   4

The "80" Percent Rule

Case Type:	Data Case
Main Subjects:	Discrimination, Diversity, Recruiting/Selection
Who's Who:	• Betty Chu, *Human Resources Manager*
	• Jennifer Ortiz, *Restaurant Manager*

E-mail Messages

Hi Betty,

   I enjoyed our diversity meeting last week. If my memory serves me correctly, you mentioned that there is a practical device to see if we unintentionally discriminate against a group of people.

   Regards,
   Jennifer

Hi Jennifer,

   Yes, the "80 Percent Rule" is a statistical measure for determining underutilization of minorities and women. According to the EEOC Uniform Guidelines, an employee selection program has been potentially discriminatory when the selection rates for any racial, ethnic, or sex class is less than four-fifths (or 80%) of the rate of the class with the highest selection rate. I will attach some data for you. Let's discuss your results at our next diversity meeting.

   —Betty

1. Based on the data in Exhibit 4.1, determine if the restaurant's selection procedure has been potentially discriminatory according to this rule.

2. What actions can companies consider when adverse impact is indicated in the selection process?

EXHIBIT 4.1

Hiring Information—Royal Hotel Restaurant Servers

Over the last 5 years 150 people applied for restaurant server position at the Royal Hotel.

GROUP	APPLIED	SELECTED
Female	50	14
Male	100	52

Notes and Responses to Case Questions:

Case 5

The Left-Handed Server

Case Type:	**Head Case**
Main Subjects:	**Discrimination, Diversity, Recruiting/Selection**
Who's Who:	• Thomas Waxer, *Banquet Manager*

The Royal Hotel offers its banquet guests a very formal type of service called Silver or Russian service. Thomas believes in consistency and elegance. He often admires servers as they line up in the ballroom of the Royal, all carrying serving platters in the same manner. He is convinced that guests value this consistency and grace.

When Thomas has a doubt if potential candidates have gained enough experience in banquet service, he puts them through what he calls a "work sampling" test. This consists of carrying plates, as well as portioning and serving fake food directly onto ten plates arranged on a round banquet table. He scores each candidate's performance on a scale of "A" to "F." Those with a score of "C" or less are eliminated.

This morning, while testing a candidate, Thomas noticed that he was carrying the platter with his right hand. "This is not correct," Thomas told him. "Did you read the job description?" Thomas pointed to the printed information material on the position (see Exhibit 5.1). The server replied, "I'm truly sorry Sir. I can't transfer the food with my right hand. I was allowed to serve like this back in my country."

1. What are the advantages and disadvantages of work sampling tests?

2. What are some of the pitfalls of Thomas's preemployment test?

3. Should Thomas force left-handed servers to carry platters with their left hand and portion the food with their right hand?

Reference

The Culinary Institute of America. (2001). *Remarkable Service* (pp. 185–192). New York: Wiley.

EXHIBIT 5.1

Information Material

Job Description—Banquet Server

Key responsibilities:

Serve food and/or beverages in a friendly, courteous, and professional manner according to Royal's high standards of quality.

Clear tables after service. Perform other duties as assigned, which may include assisting with set up and break down of function space and plating of meals.

Qualifications:

Ability to lift 40 pounds or more.

Strong knowledge of Russian (Silver) food service style.

Royal Hotel—Banquets Training Manual (Excerpt)

The main goal of Silver or Russian service is to service fully cooked food while it is still hot and to serve it in an elegant manner. The server stands with feet together, to the left of the guest. Food is plated with the aid of a serving spoon and fork with the server's right hand. Servers move counterclockwise around the table.

Considerable skill, strength, and dexterity are required to perform proper platter service. Trays can be heavy and hot and must be held firmly in the left hand while the food is being served with the right hand from the guest's left. Practice is required to prevent dropping or breaking the food or spilling the sauce.

Notes and Responses to Case Questions:

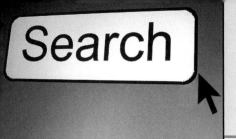

The On-Line Dirt

Case Type:	**Head Case**
Main Subjects:	**Discrimination, Recruiting/Selection**
Who's Who:	• Betty Chu, *Human Resources Manager*
	• Katherine Norton, *Director of Human Resources*

"Betty, let's conduct our usual social media background check on this promising candidate," smiled Katherine. "Make a decision this afternoon; give him a call and set up his interview for Monday. By the way, I am going to take off now; I need to do some shopping for the holiday party," Katherine added as she left the HR office.

Once Katherine had left, Betty went on-line to check on the candidate for an open management position. At one of the popular social networking sites, she found the candidate's personal Web page with the description of his main interests: "Sand, sun, and sex." In addition, Betty found a few mildly provocative pictures taken recently at a college party. One of them was portraying the candidate in underwear drinking from a half-pint beer mug.

1. Many companies are using search engines to conduct virtual background checks on candidates. What are the pros of this practice?

2. What are the risks involved of going on-line to research job candidates?

3. If you were Betty, what would you do now?

References

Finder, A. (2006, June 11). *For some, online persona undermines a resume.* Retrieved December 7, 2007 from http://www.nytimes.com

Notes and Responses to Case Questions:

C a s e   7

Unexpected Interview

Case Type:	**Application Case**
Main Subject:	**Recruiting/Selection**
Who's Who:	• Betty Chu, *Human Resources Manager*
	• Judith Grace, *Front Office Manager*
	• Julie Hill, *Assistant Front Office Manager*

J ulie, the new assistant front office manager, was about to leave for the day
when she received an e-mail from Betty, the Human Resources manager:

Hi Julie,

Hope you enjoyed your orientation session last week. Judith has
preselected some candidates to be interviewed for the front desk agent
position. I set up five interviews for you for tomorrow morning. Please find
the job ad we placed on www.excellenthoteljobs.com attached[1]. Would you
be so kind as to put together a set of behavioral-based[2] questions?

I am sure the required competencies[3] can easily be identified. I am sorry, we
don't have a structured interview system in place as of yet. You know we don't
have any corporate support.

Sorry for this last-minute request.

Best,

Notes

[1]See Exhibit 7.1.

[2]An interview technique focuses on a candidate's past experiences, behaviors, knowledge, skills, and
abilities by asking the candidate to provide specific examples of when he or she has demonstrated
certain behaviors or skills as a means of predicting future behavior and performance.

[3]A competency is a cluster of related knowledge, skills, abilities, and other personal characteristics
(KSAOs) working together to produce outstanding performance in a given area of responsibility. In
selection systems, a competency model ensures that all interviewers are looking for the same set of
attributes.

Attachment

THE ROYAL HOTEL
•••
FRONT DESK AGENT
•••

Do you have a proactive nature and an "I can help you" attitude?

The front desk agent is responsible for delighting our guest—whatever it takes—right from the start to the end of their stay. This fast-paced and highly visible role gives opportunity for casual conversation and has a direct impact on creating the guest experience.

Responsibilities and job functions include but are not limited to the following:

- Promptly and effectively deal with guest's requests
- Work closely with the housekeeping department in keeping room status reports up-to date and coordinates requests for maintenance and repair work
- Manage and resolve all guest complaints in a professional and courteous manner
- Initiate and monitor shift checklist for proper completion of tasks
- Responsible for cash drawer contents and transactions during shift
- Ensure that the front desk and back office is clean and well organized.

E-mail: hr@royalhotel.com

---

1. Identify approximately 10 competencies required for a successful front desk agent at the Royal Hotel.

2. Prepare the interview with appropriate questions.

3. What are the pros and cons of the behavioral-based interviewing technique?

Notes and Responses to Case Questions:

Case 8

The Incomplete Schedule

Case Type:	Data Case
Main Subjects:	Controlling Costs, Productivity
Who's Who:	• Judith Grace, *Front Office Manager*
	• Dan Mazur, *Director of Rooms*
	• Jane Peterson, *Hotel Manager*
	• Marina Wright, *Revenue Manager*

J
udith had a crazy day. The Royal was fully booked and she had only five minutes to look at the forecast and put together the schedule for the first week of December. Before leaving the hotel she slid the document under the door of the Director of rooms. Judith was already making her tea at home when she received a voice mail from Dan.

Voice Mail

"Hi Judith, this is Dan speaking. Thanks for submitting your schedule for next week. Unfortunately, you missed Tuesday. To help you, I called Marina who gave me some information. Alright! Monday's occupancy will be 200 rooms, some of them, I guess 135, will check out on Tuesday. According to Marina, Tuesday night the hotel occupancy will be 240 rooms.

Would you mind leaving me a quick message with the missing information? Please keep in mind that Jane would like to review all schedules today.

Thanks, bye."

The Royal Hotel developed labor productivity standards[1] for each department. Judith knew that the Front Desk could use eight hours per shift (A.M., P.M., Overnight), regardless of the occupancy. She also remembered that their labor productivity standards were based on the number of arrivals and departures. Above 100 arrivals and departures, she was entitled to include another eight hours for the day. When arrivals and departures exceeded 150, she could add another shift. Finally, above 300 arrivals and departures, she could schedule one more agent shift.

1. What are some of the challenges a hospitality organization may face when creating productivity standards?

2. What are the implications if too many employees are scheduled?

3. Could you help Judith out by determining how many front desk agent hours she can schedule for Tuesday, December 2?

Notes

[1]LABOR PRODUCTIVITY STANDARDS

Productivity is the number of hours needed to service a hospitality unit.
Labor standards utilize productivity ratios to identify the ideal amount of labor (including fixed and variable labor hours) to service incremental volumes of hospitality business.
Labor standards serve as day-to-day operational guidelines, helping managers to stay within budgetary guidelines.

References

Heath, D. (2002). *A case in labor management.* Retrieved December 22, 2007, from the HFTP Web site: http://www.hftp.org/members/bottomline/backissues/2002/BL17_3/case.htm

Thompson, G. M. (1998). Labor scheduling, part 2. *Cornell Hotel and Restaurant Administration Quarterly, 39*(6), 26–37.

Notes and Responses to Case Questions:

Image © Viktor1, 2009. Used under license from Shutterstock.com

The Bartender's Break

Case Type:	**Head Case**
Main Subjects:	ADA, Flexibility, Job Design/Job Description, Productivity
Who's Who:	• Matthew Knorr, *Director of Food and Beverage*
	• Emily Perkins, *Lounge and Bar Manager*
	• Kalman Rosen, *Barback*

"I need a little bit of assistance," Emily said when she called the Food and Beverage office. Matthew ran down to the Lounge.

"We have to send the bartender on break; could you watch the door for me?" Emily asked him.

As a "hands-on" manager, Matthew was happy to help out on the floor. He was, however, surprised that while Emily was making drinks behind the bar, the barback, Kalman, was chatting with a customer and they were watching the ball game together on the flat screen TV placed behind the bar.

P.M. bartenders had a first dinner break covered by the A.M. bartenders, and they were also entitled to a shorter 15-minute break in the evening. Traditionally, managers were replacing the bartenders during the second break. Matthew believed that managers should be on the floor at all times to ensure that service is flawless; he could not understand why Kalman was not able to cover for the bartender.

The next day, Emily and Matthew met Kalman to discuss the issue. After praising the barback's overall performance, Matthew asked him to cover the bartender's second break starting next week. "You have been with the Royal Hotel for five years; I am sure you want to learn new skills and take on more challenging assignments." Matthew added. "Sorry, Matthew, I am just not interested in covering the bartender's break. I am happy with what I am doing right now. By the way," Kalman added politely, "that's not even in my job description." Matthew reminded the barback that job descriptions are not meant to be all-inclusive and jobs are subject to change and pointed to the disclaimer on the barback's job description:

"Other duties and responsibilities may be assigned."

"You know, Kalman, that nothing in this job description restricts my right to reassign duties and responsibilities to you. Let's meet again tomorrow to finalize this." Matthew ended the discussion.

1. List some of the positive and negative impacts of using job descriptions.
2. Evaluate Matthew's actions in dealing with the situation. What factors should he consider in his decision?

EXHIBIT 9.1

JOB DESCRIPTION—Bartender

Title: Bartender

Department: The riverside lounge and bar

Report To: Lounge and bar manager

Position Summary: Mixes and serves alcoholic and nonalcoholic drinks and food items to patrons of bar in a prompt and courteous manner.

ESSENTIAL JOB FUNCTIONS:
- Knows all food and beverage items and daily specials, and communicates them to the guest.
- Takes orders from customers, using upselling techniques.
- Mixes ingredients to prepare cocktails and other drinks.
- Rings guest checks; collects money for food and drinks served.
- Closes guest checks by credit cards, cash, or room charges, according to Royal operating procedures.
- Orders or requisitions liquors and supplies.
- Maintains a clean and efficient bar, both in and out of customer view.
- Monitors guest behavior and guest alcohol consumption to determine when alcohol service to the guest should cease.

ADDITIONAL RESPONSIBILITIES:
- Other duties and responsibilities may be assigned.

MINIMUM QUALIFICATIONS:
- High school diploma preferred.

THIS JOB REQUIRES ABILITY TO PERFORM THE FOLLOWING:
- Handling, carrying, or pushing items weighing up to 50 pounds.
- Extensive periods of standing.
- Bending, stooping, kneeling, and lifting.

LICENSES OR CERTIFICATES REQUIRED:
- Health/food handler cards as required by state government agency.
- Alcohol Awareness Certification.
- Must meet state legal age requirements.

EXHIBIT 9.2

JOB DESCRIPTION—Barback

Title: Barback

Department: The riverside lounge and bar

Report To: Lounge and bar manager

Position Summary: Responsible for ensuring the quick and efficient servicing of the bar and lounge while providing excellent service.

ESSENTIAL JOB FUNCTIONS:

- Assists bartenders as directed; prepares garnishes and mixes.
- Replenishes supplies throughout shift.
- Familiar with all food and beverage items, as well daily specials to respond accurately to any guest inquiry.
- Retrieves food orders from kitchen and delivers them to the bar.
- Maintains a clean and efficient bar, both in and out of customer view.

ADDITIONAL RESPONSIBILITIES:

- Other duties and responsibilities may be assigned.

MINIMUM QUALIFICATIONS:

- No formal education required.

THIS JOB REQUIRES ABILITY TO PERFORM THE FOLLOWING:

- Handling, carrying, or pushing items weighing up to 50 pounds.
- Extensive periods of standing.
- Bending, stooping, kneeling, and lifting.

LICENSES OR CERTIFICATES REQUIRED:

- Health/food handler cards as required by state government agency.
- Must meet state legal age requirements.

Notes and Responses to Case Questions:

Building Your Leadership Credibility

Image © VR Photos, 2009. Used under license from Shutterstock.com

Kitchen Camaraderie

Case Type:	**Head Case**
Main Subjects:	**Recruiting/Selection, Self-Confidence**
Who's Who:	• Pascal Gateau, *Executive Chef*
	• Lori Grafton, *Food and Beverage Assistant*
	• Matthew Knorr, *Director of Food and Beverage*

The topic of the Food and Beverage (F&B) meeting today was the importance of camaraderie. Chef Gateau was enthusiastic about the subject and shared his view with other managers. Lori, the F&B assistant, kindly took notes and placed the draft meeting minutes on Matthew's desk. Here are some of the comments, the chef made:

FOOD QUALITY

I have total control over how I run my kitchen.

The ingredients are the star of my dishes.

I get great compliments for my dishes.

I feel like my cooking is instinctive cooking.

My plates are so hot that when you touch them, you are going to need a napkin.

CREATING A TEAM

I hire and promote people who complement me and have strengths where I need it.

I spend much time and energy to build my team.

My team sees me as a strong member of the team.

I run my kitchen as a group effort and push my vision of perfection.

My team is dedicated and focused.

If I want my cooks to do their best work, I must supply them with the best ingredients.

I encourage my team to develop a habit of increasing guest interaction.

CLOSING COMMENT

My advice for new employees is, don't let your ego get in the way.

The chef's performance appraisal was coming up and Matthew definitely wanted to highlight areas of improvements.

1. What advice would you give Matthew?
2. Imagine that you are interviewing potential candidates who are systematically avoiding the word "I" when you ask them to speak about their past achievements. How would these applicants sound to you?

References

This case is inspired by situations described in:

Wilder, J. (2005, August). Kitchen camaraderie. *Santé, 9*(5), 32.

Notes and Responses to Case Questions:

Off The Record

Case Type:	Head Case
Main Subjects:	Harassment, Open-Door Policy, Trust
Who's Who:	• Paul Bello, *Purchasing Manager*
	• Anisa Schumacher, *Purchasing Agent*
	• Corey Widman, *Bellman*

"May I have a confidential meeting with you?" asked Anisa, one of the purchasing agents. "Sure," answered Paul Bello; and he invited Anisa into his small office next to the loading dock. "Please don't say anything to anyone," Anisa said.

"No worries," smiled Paul. "This will be between you and me; you have my word on this."

"This is about Corey, the bellman," continued Anisa. "He is harassing me, but I don't want anyone to know about the situation … . I'm in a family crisis situation," Anisa added and started to cry hysterically. Paul's hands got sweaty and he really did not know what to say now that Anisa had confided in him.

1. Is Paul obligated to honor this kind of employee request? Explain.

2. What should Paul have done differently?

3. Assume that you are Paul and an employee from the Food and Beverage division is requesting a confidential meeting with you. What would be your response in that case?

Notes and Responses to Case Questions:

Image © Uranov, 2009. Used under license from Shutterstock.com

Don't Shoot
The Messenger

Case Type:	Issue Case
Main Subjects:	Buy-In, Change, Credibility, Influence, Unpopular Decisions
Who's Who:	• Shakia Andrews, *Executive Housekeeper*
	• Angelica Hoang, *Housekeeper*
	• Dan Mazur, *Director of Rooms*

The Housekeeping department held an unusually well-attended meeting. Most of the time was dedicated to the new policy recently introduced by management. According to the new procedure, housekeepers are required to ensure that dirty room service carts do not remain in the hotel corridors. From now on they will be asked to push the carts down to the back landings, located on each guest floor.

Heated words were exchanged as many housekeepers expressed anger and concern about the additional workload. "I hear you guys. I am on your side. But you know how it is; he didn't allow me to do what I wanted … welcome to the Royal Hotel!" smiled Shakia, while gesturing toward the second floor where Dan's office is. Angelica, one of the long-standing housekeepers, tried to calm the others in a surprisingly compassionate tone of voice. "Ladies, please don't shoot the messenger; Shakia is not responsible for this new procedure."

1. Evaluate Shakia's actions in dealing with the situation. How do you explain her behavior?

2. How do you think employees perceive Shakia as a manager?

3. If you were in charge, how would you have handled the implementation of this new procedure?

Notes and Responses to Case Questions:

Image © mypokcik, 2009. Used uncer license from Shutterstock.com

Passing The Buck

Case Type:	Issue Case
Main Subjects:	Authority, Big Picture, Delegation, Flexibility, Hands-On, Influence, Self-Confidence
Who's Who:	• Matthew Knorr, *Director of Food and Beverage*
	• Robert Kunz, *General Manager*
	• Emily Perkins, *Lounge and Bar Manager*
	• Louise Rausch, *Director of Finance*

Robert Kunz was wondering why Matthew was late for the executive committee meeting. "Sorry, I am late; we had a crunch situation in the Lounge. Emily asked me to cover the door for her. I also took some orders and cleared tables. We all worked together as a team. I think everybody felt good about the outcome," Matthew was excited as he explained the situation.

"That's what happened last week," mumbled Kunz to himself, and turned to Matthew.

"Do you see the big picture?" Kunz asked slowly. Matthew was somewhat puzzled and unconsciously glanced at the big picture hanging on the wall showing the scenic Bedford River in winter.

"Alright," said the General Manager as he changed the subject, "Matthew is exhausted; let's have a coffee first."

While sipping the coffee, Matthew was wondering what Kunz's was referring to. He believed that he was able to gain the confidence of most of the staff through his hands-on approach. True, he thought, over the last few months he had been spending lots of time with Emily. Already twice this week, Matthew remembered, Emily had stopped by his office and asked for his assistance. In both cases, she approached him with the same verbiage: "I just want to run this by you…. I know you're the expert…. I really respect your judgment." Although, Matthew believed that Emily should have been able to handle those bar inventory issues by herself, he literally dropped everything and helped her.

"Should we work a little bit?" Kunz asked finally and had Louise hand out a copy of the latest P/L statement to everyone.

1. What are the pros and cons of managers being highly engaged in the day-to-day operation?
2. What problems do you see concerning Matthew's effectiveness as a manager?
3. Highlight reasons why employees attempt upward delegation.
4. Identify techniques managers can use to prevent reverse delegation.
5. How can managers "get the big picture"?

Notes and Responses to Case Questions:

Image © Marcin Balcerzak, 2009. Used under license from Shutterstock.com

The Flashbacks

Case Type:	**Incident Case**
Main Subjects:	**Assertiveness, Authority, Coaching, Feedback, Incivility, Influence, Meetings, Organizational Structure, Rapport**
Who's Who:	• Shakia Andrews, *Executive Housekeeper*
	• Lori Canelle, *Spa Manager*
	• Carlos Diaz, *Guest Services Manager*
	• Judit Grace, *Front Office Manager*
	• Robert Kunz, *General Manager*
	• Dan Mazur, *Director of Rooms*
	• Kalinda Stenton, *PBX Manager*
	• Marina Wright, *Revenue Manager*

D an couldn't fall asleep. Just a bad day! First of all, the Rooms Division meeting, with a full agenda, started twenty minutes late this afternoon, as Mr. Kunz stopped by and was casually speaking about various topics. "And that joke," Dan remembered. "Stop me if you've heard the latest joke," said Kunz turning to the group. "The trouble with being a leader," he started. "I know," Marina interrupted, "is that you can't be sure whether people are following you or chasing you," she finished with a chuckle. No one else was laughing, and at once everybody in the room became silent. Kunz was finally paged by the front desk and left the meeting.

That was just the start! Overall, Dan did not feel that the entire meeting went well, and he kept having flashbacks about various parts of the meeting. He was constantly pondering what would be the best way to deal with similar occurrences in the future.

Flashback 1

At a previous Rooms Division meeting, Dan assigned a short, five-minute report on a specific topic to each department head. At today's meeting Kalinda was scheduled to present her findings. However, Kalinda prepared not only the report but a longer PowerPoint presentation and had demanded from Dan, during the meeting, more time to present the slides to the managers. Dan was caught completely off guard.

Flashback 2

Shakia gave a brief overview on cleaning supplies that included a transparency about how well Housekeeping managed this expense line. Dan noticed a calculation error that entirely changed the accuracy of Shakia's data. The department actually spent more money than was budgeted. Dan politely mentioned the mistake. Marina also pointed out a small spelling error on the transparency. Shakia was visibly outraged.

Flashback 3

After Shakia finished her overview, Lori asked her numerous questions about what cleaning supplies she should use to disinfect the sauna.

Flashback 4

Judith spoke rarely and avoided eye contact; she was clearly not used to participating in discussions.

"Let's hear now from Judith," Dan prompted her in the middle of the meeting. She blushed and felt she was being put on the spot and was unable to contribute.

Flashback 5

Everybody knew that Carlos and Lori disliked each other. In the past, Carlos often tried to make Lori look like a fool. While addressing the issue of setting up a crunch team, Lori suggested that Carlos should cross train all employees on how to park a car. He answered Lori that her idea was really brainless and he did not have the extra money to pay for the training hours. Lori got defensive and commented in detail on Carlos's questionable organizational skills during peak hours.

Flashback 6

The team was obviously struggling with the mystery shopper report follow-up.

Dan was seeking some consensus on whether the Rooms Division should involve other managers as well to perform regular room spot checks. However, the department heads were unable to reach a decision and the group was unclear about what steps to take next. Dan was desperately looking for the right way to refocus the group's energy and attention.

Flashback 7

Kalinda suggested that to improve the level of service, guests should be asked if they wished their wake-up calls to be delivered in English, Spanish, or possibly in other languages. "Kalinda, this is not a very useful idea," Dan told her. At this point, the banquet houseman came in and asked if he could start setting up the room for dinner.

EXHIBIT 14.1

Royal Hotel
ROOMS DIVISION MEETING—AGENDA
Bedford Meeting Room
WEDNESDAY, JANUARY 14, 2009.
2 P.M.
1. Overview of Year 2008—DAN
2. The Floor is Yours—KALINDA
3. Cleaning Supplies—SHAKIA
4. Developing a Crunch Plan for Guest Services—Brainstorming
5. Mystery Shopper Report Follow-up
6. New Business

---

1. Do you agree with the following statement? *Incivility in meetings is affected by status. Those with greater power have more ways to be uncivil and get away with it.* Please explain.

2. A variety of situations can arise when you chair a meeting.
   a. Identify the issues that are present in this case.
   b. What recommendations would you give to Dan in terms of addressing each issue effectively in the future?

3. Assume that Marina is too talkative in the meeting. How would you cut her off?

4. What general observations can be made to prevent such situations from reoccurring?

References

Bielous, G. (1996, June). Five ways to cope with difficult people. *SuperVision, 57*(6), 14–16.

Cava, R. (2004). *Dealing with Difficult People* (pp. 176–180). Buffalo, NY: Firefly Books.

Hamlin, S. (2005). *How to Talk So People Listen* (pp. 263–295). New York: HarperCollins Publishers.

Lilley, R. (2002). *Dealing with Difficult People* (pp. 125–137). London: Kogan Page.

Ramsey, R. D. (2000, October). Watch how you talk about your job. *SuperVision, 63*(10), 17–19.

Stone, F. (2003). *The Manager's Question and Answer Book* (pp. 76–95). New York: Amacom.

Notes and Responses to Case Questions:

Image © Yuri Arcurs, 2009. Used under license from
Shutterstock.com

Case 15

The Morning Fun

Case Type:	Incident Case
Main Subjects:	Harassment, Humor/Sarcasm
Who's Who:	• Jane Peterson, *Hotel Manager*
	• Brian White, *Assistant Director of Engineering*

Jane often started her meetings with a quick "life lesson." "I believe that laughter can make a difference. Humor lowers stress and promotes teamwork. When it comes to hiring employees, the Royal Hotel is always looking for people with a good sense of humor." This is how Jane started the safety meeting today.

"I have a joke" said Brian from Engineering. At this point he started to explain to the audience, "the top 10 reasons why a handgun is better than a woman." Everyone was laughing in the room, including Jane. She looked around and said, "That's what I said! Fun boosts performance. No other female is in the room and I'm not offended at all. Let's review the monthly accidents."

1. Evaluate the situation. What might be some of the issues in this case?

2. List those topics that you can joke about in the workplace. What are the subjects and situations that should be avoided?

3. Should the Royal management take any action?

Notes and Responses to Case Questions:

The Juice Squeezer

Case Type:	Issue Case
Main Subjects:	Assertiveness, Big-Picture, Buy-In, Change, Controlling Costs, Decision Making, Respect, Unpopular Decisions, Trust
Who's Who:	• Wesley Edwards, *Room Service Manager* • Matthew Knorr, *Director of Food and Beverage* • Nick Willems, *Room Service Server*

Wesley's last performance appraisal indicated that he needs to work on his people skills. He knew that trust and respect must be earned over time, with repeated experience. Therefore, he was happy when Room Service servers recently approached him with their idea of making fresh orange juice in the guest rooms. The employees' spokesperson, Nick, even showed Wesley a manual juice squeezer in a catalog, and explained, "This will enhance the customers' value perception and we can make more tips." Unbeknownst to the servers, the Royal hotel recently decided to purchase freshly squeezed orange juice from a local company, which was delivered every morning, to save money. Wesley was therefore hesitant with his answer. Seeing this, Nick said with disappointment in his voice, "You guys just don't respect us and our ideas." Deep inside, Wesley disliked Nick and didn't believe that he should be part of the Royal team.

Earlier that morning Wesley had already made an appointment with Matthew to discuss the growing number of timing-related guest complaints and ways of keeping Food and Beverage (F&B) costs within budgetary guidelines.

Even though he had doubts about the viability of the employees' suggestion, he decided to further discuss the juice squeezer with Matthew. The F&B director carefully listened while Wesley explained the idea to him. At the end, the F&B director looked at Wesley somewhat annoyed and said, "As much as I appreciate that you shared this with me, I am more interested to hear what you told your team about their suggestion." When Wesley remained silent, Matthew suggested that he would get back to the employees.

1. Can managers respect those employees they mistrust or dislike?

2. Identify behaviors promoting and undermining trust in the following areas:
    *   Interpersonal Skills
    *   Fairness/Consistency
    *   Decision-Making Process
    *   Information Flow
    *   Achievements/Mistakes
    *   Feedback/Criticism
    *   Problem and Conflict Resolution

3. How do you think Wesley's willingness to address his team's idea with Matthew, will further earn the employees' respect?

4. What problems might Matthew see concerning Wesley's effectiveness as a manager?

Notes and Responses to Case Questions:

The Service Elevator

Case Type:	**Application Case**
Main Subjects:	**Anger, Assertiveness, Buy-In, Change, Rapport, Unpopular Decisions, Team Building**
Who's Who:	• Carlos Diaz, *Guest Services Manager*
	• Matthew Knorr, *Director of Food and Beverage*
	• Dan Mazur, *Director of Rooms*

C arlos was furious at Dan. He swore at him and yelled, "That's the stupidest thing I've ever seen! How could you do something like that?" He slammed his fist against his desk, the vein in his temple pulsating, "Answer me! How could you do something so stupid?"

Every morning at the Royal Hotel, during heavy checkout periods, one of the service elevators was reserved for bell attendants so that they can efficiently transport luggage from guest rooms to the front door area. Yesterday, after lengthy discussion, Dan and Matthew agreed that Room Service would be using this elevator because the hotel had been receiving a large number of complaints as a result of breakfast delivery delays.

Dan turned to Carlos and said to him, "Your behavior is not appropriate here at work," but the Guest Service manager was so angry that he couldn't even hear him.

1. How do you think Dan should deal with Carlos?

   a. Use the seven steps outlined in Exhibit 17.1 to identify some options/ strategies for Dan.

   b. Be creative. Where appropriate identify statements Dan could use.

EXHIBIT 17.1

Royal Hotel—Management Handbook (excerpts)

DEALING WITH ANGER

You goal is not to get rid of anger—it's to help the other person express his or her anger more calmly, so the two of you can solve the problem. When someone is angry with you, these skills can help you lower the intensity of the person's anger.

A. DECIDING WHETHER THE OTHER PERSON REALLY WANTS TO WORK THINGS OUT WITH YOU

Although we like to assume that the other person does want to work things out, it's possible that the person is too emotional at the moment to want to work on it. To gain the other person's cooperation and willingness to do his or her part of the work, occasionally you may have to get upper management's help.

B. BEING DIRECT

Being direct means:

Talking to the right person.

Being specific and making clear what are your goals or purposes.

C. ACKNOWLEDGING FEELINGS

Acknowledge the anger, talk about it, listen to the person experiencing it, and validate it—before you try to talk about the facts or other issues. The angry person will be calmer and more reasonable if he or she first has a chance to be heard.

D. FINDING SOMETHING IN COMMON

When someone is angry with you, thinking about what you have in common can help prepare you to talk to the person about the issue.

E. DEPERSONALIZING

A major source of anger and conflict is taking things too personally. To depersonalize, you must ask yourself whether what you heard (or think you heard) is related to work, or whether it is a personal attack. If it is related to work, focus on the work issue involved and disregard the personal references.

F. IDENTIFYING THE REAL ISSUES

The key—once feelings are acknowledged and common ground is established—you can get to the real issues. Getting to the real issues helps you move past misinterpretations, vague impressions, and assumptions and enables you to deal with the facts.

G. LETTING GO

In anger and conflict, the need to let go means that, even though you've taken all the above steps, you still can't make the other person do what you want and you can't make things turn out the way you want. What you've done is allow for what you want to happen—and the response is in the other person's hands.

References

This case is based on the principles and situations described in:

McClure, L. (2000). *Anger and Conflict in the Workplace*. Manassas Park, VA: Impact Publications.

Notes and Responses to Case Questions:

Image © Rob Marmion, 2009. Used under license from Shutterstock.com

Claudia's Training Assignment

Case Type:	**Application Case**
Main Subjects:	**Assertiveness, Defensiveness, Feedback, Rapport**
Who's Who:	• Shakia Andrews, *Executive Housekeeper*
	• Claudia Kawata, *Management Trainee*
	• Manuel Mercadante, *Houseman*
	• Mary Sims, *Catering Coordinator*
	• Kelly Woodstock, *Catering Manager*

Six months ago, Claudia was hired to be part of the Royal Management Training Program. This was a self-paced, individual program designed to provide candidates with the leadership skills necessary to become entry-level managers. The key component of this program was rotating through just about every department at the Royal Hotel. As part of the schedule, Claudia had to perform a variety of learning activities. According to the training guideline, this month she had to focus on developing coaching abilities. Today, she had to complete some assignments on "Delivering Constructive Feedback."

Starting next week Claudia will attend a one-week classroom session to recap the material she had covered over the first six months. Let's assist her.

1. CLAUDIA! THESE ARE THE DISCUSSION QUESTIONS FOR YOUR CLASSROOM TRAINING SESSION NEXT WEEK:

   a. Many people resist critical feedback; receivers are likely to disagree with critiques. Please explain.

   b. Employees need to receive feedback regarding their performance. At the same time, feedback often results in performance declines. Why? To explain, please consider the following areas:

   • Feedback's focus and purpose
   • Number of sources

- Individual factors—employee
- Individual factors—supervisor
- Organizational factors

2. WRITTEN ASSIGNMENT A—COMMUNICATION PATTERNS

- Please review the following managerial statements. Identify mistakes and, if necessary, suggest an alternative approach for the managers that build rapport.
- Recommend alternative employee answers as well for the mini-scenario only. Be creative.
- Please read Exhibit 18.1 before starting this exercise.

STATEMENT	YOUR COMMENTS	ALTERNATIVE MANAGERIAL APPROACH
M: You are doing an amazing job here at the Royal, but I am concerned about your work on this project.		
M: (handing a folder to the employee) This doesn't work. The memorandum needs fixing.		
Mini-Scenario M: I can't believe you haven't done the schedule. E: I am in the middle of doing some other stuff. M: Great! This is what we call the Royal attitude. E: Sorry, I'm busy; this is my eighth consecutive shift. M: Well, welcome to the hotel industry. E: I do my best. M: I warn you, your annual appraisal is coming up.		
M: Look at this table setup. Only a very sloppy person would accept it. I'm being very reasonable about this.		
M: You must remember that …		
M: (watching the employee while talking to a guest on the phone) You really have an attitude problem.		
M: (glancing at the employee's desk) You're really disorganized.		
M: You're well organized.		
M: You're aggressive.		
M: You're confident.		

(continues)

(continued)

STATEMENT	YOUR COMMENTS	ALTERNATIVE MANAGERIAL APPROACH
M: It's not professional to show up late.		
M: I'm happy to see that your work is getting better.		
M: Your presentation was well received.		
M: You have been showing disrespect for Mike again.		
E: (sharing his medical condition) M: Well, over fifty this can happen. I'm sorry!		
M: You never complete work on deadline.		

M: Manager
E: Employee

3. WRITTEN ASSIGNMENT B—COMMUNICATION PATTERNS

    You witnessed that the following statement was made by Shakia, a Royal manager:
    "Manuel is not a team player. I need to sit down with him." Assume that you serve as Shakia's coach. Identify and ask her a few questions in order to make her feedback session with Manuel a successful one. (Please review the concepts in Exhibit 18.1 again.)

4. WRITTEN ASSIGNMENT C—INTERPERSONAL STYLES

    You are Kelly, the Catering manager. You have drafted a long and rather complicated wedding proposal for an important client. You have agreed with Mary, the Catering coordinator, that it will be ready at four o'clock to allow time for last-minute changes. It is now half past four and there is still no sign of the proposal. Identify a passive, an aggressive, and an assertive way of approaching the coordinator.
    Please review Exhibit 18.2 before starting this exercise.

5. WRITTEN ASSIGNMENT D—ASSISTING TECHNIQUES

    •   Please review the following managerial statements. Suggest solutions that build rapport.
    •   Please read Exhibit 18.3 before starting this exercise.

STATEMENT	SUGGESTED SOLUTION
"YOU" And "I" Statements	
M: When you interrupt me, you are being rude.	M:
M: You let me down.	M:
Closed and Open Questions	
M: Why did you do that?	M:
M: Surely you can recognize the error, can't you?	M:
Paraphrasing	
E: I am overloaded. I have too many assignments.	M:
Mirroring	
E: Honestly, I've had it! The hotel is bombarding me with new assignments to the point where there's no way I can finish the shift report.	M:
E: I'm doing twice as much work Mary is, and it's unfair.	M:
Reframing	
E: You're sneaky! I can't believe that you brought this up to Dan behind my back.	M:
Higher-up M: You're a slacker and you're not pulling your weight here at the Royal.	M:

M: Manager
E: Employee

EXHIBITS

Royal Hotel—Management Training Manual (Excerpts)

Delivering Constructve Feedback

The way managers deliver feedback strongly influences its effectiveness. Presented below are guidelines intended for effective feedback.

EXHIBIT 18.1

COMMUNICATION PATTERNS
- We can identify multiple patterns in interpersonal relationships.
- As depicted below, the continua allow for a more complex understanding of responses we give and receive in the workplace. Senders and receivers move from one stage to another along each continuum.
- The usage of the nine communication continua is often simultaneous. These overlapping patterns weaken or strengthen each other.

(continues)

EXHIBIT 18.1 (CONTINUED)

CORRECTIVE  REASSURING

Corrective feedback is a response that tells an employee what they are doing wrong.
(Focus on mistakes)

Reassuring feedback encourages the employees to be open to further improvement.
(Focus on job well done)

DEFENSIVE  SUPPORTIVE

Defensive Behaviors

- Messages carry judgments and evaluation of others or their ideas.
- These attempt to control the conversation or situation.
- Messages suggest the speaker is trying to direct others.
- Messages demonstrate lack of interest or indifference.
- No room for differing ideas or viewpoints.

When a defensive communication style is used, the receiver most often responds defensively.

Supportive Behaviors

- Messages are clear, specific statements without loaded words or judgmental cues.
- A problem orientation that is not imposing.
- The speaker's talk is unplanned and free of hidden motives.
- Messages convey interest and understanding, responsive to other's feelings and thoughts.
- Equality based on mutual trust and respect.

A supportive climate is built on understanding. When using this style of communication, a manager is concerned and willing to listen to the explanation offered by the subordinate.

SUPERIORITY  EQUALITY

Superiority

One source of defensive climate is the superior nature of messages.

Equality

To promote a sense of equality, the supervisor must convey mutual respect.

SOLUTION GIVING  PROBLEM INQUIRY

Solution Giving

When giving feedback, the manager provides solutions without discussing/exploring the actual problem.

Problem Inquiry

The emphasis in problem inquiry is placed on assisting employees to find a problem's solution.

EVALUATIVE/JUDGMENTAL  DESCRIPTIVE

Evaluative/Judgmental

Responses are evaluative when they are phrased with labels such as good, bad, right or wrong. Evaluative feedback is likely to cause a defensive reaction.

Descriptive

The manager is focusing on particular features of the work performance. This helps the employee to make concrete connections with what the supervisor is talking about.

(continues)

EXHIBIT 18.1 (CONTINUED)

GENERAL ⟵――――――――――⟶ SPECIFIC

General/Global

The vagueness makes the feedback difficult to interpret correctly. Global or blanket statements often produce defensiveness.

Specific

Unless the feedback is specific, very little learning or reinforcement is possible.

FOCUS ON ATTITUDE ⟵――――――――――⟶ FOCUS ON BEHAVIOR OR ACTIONS

Attitude

The more that feedback is molded in terms of attitude, the more it will be perceived as a personal attack and the more difficult it will be to deal with.

Behavior/Actions

Separate the people from the problem. People have total control over their own behavior. Employees may be held accountable for their actions. The more feedback is cast in terms of specific behaviors, the higher is the probability that those behaviors will be repeated.

IGNORE FEELINGS ⟵――――――――――⟶ EMPATHY

Ignore feelings

This supervisor's response disregards the apparent feelings of the employee.

Empathy

Empathic responses make employees feel understood and valued.

ABSOLUTE ⟵――――――――――⟶ CONDITIONAL

Absolute

Absolute language closes off alternative ways of interpreting the situation; there is no room for flexibility.

Conditional

Conditional language places "conditions" on statements of facts; the manager is taking into consideration various options to choose from.

Exhibit 18.1 is in part based on the information from Goodwin, C. & Griffith, D.B. (2007). *The Conflict Survival Kit: Tools for Resolving Conflict at Work* (pp. 99–111). Upper Saddle River: NJ: Pearson.

EXHIBIT 18.2

INTERPERSONAL STYLES

Every time we speak, we choose and use one of three basic communication styles: passive, assertive, and aggressive.

Passive	Assertive	Aggressive
• Passivity is not speaking up for your own rights and interests.	• Assertiveness is speaking up for your own rights and interests without violating the rights and interests of others.	• Aggressiveness is acting for your own rights and interests in a way that violates the rights and interests of others.
• Submissive people give in, even at their own expense, to avoid the discomfort of potential confrontation.	• Assertive people stand their ground; they are factual and straightforward.	• Aggressive people quickly escalate a conversation into adversarial.

EXHIBIT 18.3

ASSISTING TECHNIQUES

"YOU" AND "I" STATEMENTS

• Beginning with "You" is more likely to convey the impression that you blame the other person and that you are certain only your perceptions are correct. If the other person then responds with a "You" statement, assigning responsibility back to you, negative feelings may escalate and it may become harder to reach an understanding. In most cases, "You" messages provoke a defensive response and an argument.

• By beginning the message with "I" rather than "You," the focus is less on blaming and more on helping the receiver understand the perceptions of the feedback giver. An "I" message is an honest statement in that it discloses to the other person how you genuinely feel.

CLOSED AND OPEN QUESTIONS

Questioning has a special place in coaching. Asking good questions enables us to understand people on their own terms.

• Closed-ended questions prompt a very short, predictable answer. Closed questions tend to be straightforward, and we can use them when you want specific information. These questions generally do not lend themselves to continued conversation and may be perceived by the person being questioned as hostile or provoking.

• We can encourage the flow of information by asking more open-ended questions. An open-ended question invites a person to explain his or her point of view. They are more likely to de-escalate emotion and encourage others to "open up" and share thoughts, feelings, and opinions.

PARAPHRASING

• A paraphrase is a restatement in your own words what you think the sender is saying in his or her message. A paraphrase will demonstrate to the sender how accurately you understand the contents of a message.

• Paraphrasing helps to clarify meaning in two ways. First, by offering the speaker your version of what you've heard, you test your understanding. Second, a paraphrase demonstrates your attention and interest, thus "rewarding" the speaker and encouraging further sharing, and at a deeper level.

(continues)

EXHIBIT 18.3 (CONTINUED)

MIRRORING

- When we mirror, we hold a mirror up to the other person—describing how they look or act. We respectfully acknowledge the speaker's feelings or emotions.

- The purpose of reflecting is to let the speaker know that you understand how he or she feels about a particular topic or issue. Reflective statements are short declarative statements without indicating agreement or disagreement.

- Mirroring bad feelings helps to lower the emotional temperature.

REFRAMING

- It is difficult to maintain an attitude of curiosity and control over our emotions while we are being accused and blamed. One tool we can use as listeners is reframing. Reframing is a way of responding to a comment that changes its "frame," or subjective aspects, while maintaining its essential content.

- Statements can be reframed in ways that make them more positive, future-oriented, and much more constructive.

- Through the reframing process, we can turn negative or hostile statements into problems to be solved collaboratively.

References

Cannon, M. D., & Witherspoon, R. (2005). Actionable feedback: Unlocking the power of learning and performance improvement. *Academy of Management Executive, 19*(2), 120–134.

Collins, S. D. (2005). *Managing Conflict and Workplace Relationships* (pp. 54–55, 72–73). Mason, OH: Thomson South-Western.

Gillen, T. (1992). *Assertiveness for Managers* (p. 315). Brookfield, VT: Gower.

Goodwin, C., & Griffith, D. B. (2007). *The Conflict Survival Kit: Tools for Resolving Conflict at Work.* Upper Saddle River: NJ: Pearson.

Guilar, J. D. (2001). *The Interpersonal Communication Skills Workshop* (p. 52, pp. 69–70). New York: Amacom.

Karp, H. (2005). The lost art of feedback. In Gordon, J. (Ed.), *Pfeiffer's Classic Activities: for Developing New Managers* (pp. 251–262). Indianapolis, IN: Wiley/Pfeiffer.

Newman, D. R, & Hodgetts, R. M. (1998). *Human Resource Management: A Customer-Oriented Approach* (pp. 67–77). Upper Saddle River, NJ: Prentice Hall.

Silberman, M., & Hansburg, F. (2000). *PeopleSmart: Developing Interpersonal Intelligence* (pp. 95–117). San Francisco, CA: Berrett-Koehler Publishers, Inc.

Silverman, S. B., Pogson, C. E., & Cober, A. B. (2005). When employees at work don't get it: A model for enhancing individual employee change in response to performance feedback. *Academy of Management Executive, 18*(2), 135–147.

Sonnenschein, W. (1997). *The Diversity Toolkit* (pp. 126–128). Lincolnwood, IL: Contemporary Books.

Notes and Responses to Case Questions:

The Six Leadership Styles

Case Type:	**Application Case**
Main Subjects:	**Authority, Buy-In, Change, Coaching, Credibility, Decision Making, Influence, Leadership Styles, Trust**
Who's Who:	• Shakia Andrews, *Executive Housekeeper*

Shakia recently completed a Royal leadership seminar to learn how different leadership styles affect performance and results. She called a Housekeeping management meeting for this afternoon to explain to assistant managers the importance of being flexible and not relying on only one leadership style. To illustrate the difference between styles she came up with the following scenario:

"We are considering a new system of rotating rooms for housekeepers so that everyone gets a turn at the most expensive guest rooms and the best tips."

She closed her eyes and imagined using each of the six major leadership styles. (See Exhibit 19.1.)

1. How would you approach the housekeeping employees? For each leadership style, write a one paragraph script for Shakia. Be creative.

2. Discuss the impact that each style can have on the housekeeping work climate.

3. How do you think housekeeping employees will perceive Shakia as a manager in each of these situations?

EXHIBIT 19.1

Royal Hotel—Management Handbook (excerpt)

THE SIX LEADERSHIP STYLES

The best, most effective leaders act according to one or more of six distinct approaches to leadership and skillfully switch between the various styles depending on the situation.

	Coercive	Authoritative	Affiliative	Democratic	Pacesetting	Coaching
The leader's modus operandi	Demands immediate compliance	Mobilizes people toward a vision	Creates harmony and builds emotional bonds	Forges consensus through participation	Sets high standards for performance	Develops people for the future
The style in a phrase	"Do what I tell you."	"Come with me."	"People come first."	"What do you think?"	"Do as I do, now."	"Try this."
When the style works best	In a crisis, to kick-start a turnaround, or with problem employees	When changes require a new vision, or when a clear direction is needed	To heal rifts in a team or to motivate people during stressful circumstances	To build buy-in or consensus, or to get input from valuable employees	To get quick results from a highly motivated and competent team	To help an employee improve performance or develop long-term strengths

Notes and Responses to Case Questions:

PART THREE

Building and Managing Performance

Case 20

Sorry, I Don't Drink!

Case Type:	**Incident Case**
Main Subjects:	**Discrimination, Diversity, Performance Appraisal, Religion**
Who's Who:	• Jennifer Ortiz, *Restaurant Manager*
	• Masoud Mustafa, *Server Assistant*

Jennifer was about to finish Masoud's performance evaluation. He was one of the most efficient server assistants; he was ready to be promoted as a server.

As they discussed career plans, Jennifer told Masoud, "The only area you should really focus on now is wine knowledge. I would like to sign you up for an upcoming wine appreciation course. "I'm sorry Jennifer, I don't drink"! Masoud told her.

"But we are in the restaurant industry, you need to know about wines" Jennifer insisted.

"I'm an observant Muslim, and I would like to be a server in this five star hotel." answered Masoud quietly.

1. Do you agree with Jennifer that Masoud should have some wine knowledge?

2. Please advise Jennifer to establish career goals for Masoud.

Notes and Responses to Case Questions:

The Chef's Expertise Is Beyond My Scope!

Case Type:	**Head Case**
Main Subjects:	**Authority, Chain of Command, Feedback, Performance Appraisal, Self-Confidence**
Who's Who:	• Pascal Gateau, *Executive Chef*
	• Matthew Knorr, *Director of Food and Beverage*

A s Chef Gateau's yearly appraisal was coming up, Matthew started to worry how to conduct the discussion. The chef has much more experienced than Matthew. He had been at the Royal for ten years. He makes more money than Matthew, and most importantly his technical skills are superior. Matthew wanted to spare the embarrassment of pretending that he fully understands the technical nature of the chef's job. So, he decided that when he sits down with the chef, he will say something like "Chef, I may be the one who is in charge of doing your performance appraisal, but I realize that you have much more experience than I do. Therefore, I would like for you to tell me how you would like me to evaluate your performance." Being upfront with the chef sounded like a fair and honest approach.

The appraisal form developed for managers in culinary positions was divided into two parts:

A. *Management Skills:* (1) Integrity, (2) Direction/Decision Making, (3) Teamwork, (4) Inspire Trust, (5) Training, (6) Drive Business Result, (7) Foster Customer Focus, (8) Build Support for Change, (9) Leverage Technology.

B. *Functional Skills:* (1) Culinary Creativity and Plate Presentation, (2) Standardization of Recipes, (3) Portion Control, (4) Menu Pricing, (5) Food Purchasing, (6) Food Cost, (7) Food Inventory, (8) Sanitation Standards, (9) Proper Care of Equipment.

1. In what way do you think the chef should be treated differently when evaluating his performance?

2. What specific advice would you give Matthew to complete the two sections of the evaluation form?

3. What suggestions would you give Matthew to conduct the appraisal meeting?

4. Could you suggest performance appraisal techniques that are suitable to evaluate highly technical positions?

Reference

This case is inspired by situations described in:

Falcone, P. (Winter, 2002). *How to interview a technical candidate.* Retrieved July 10, 2007, from: http://www.shrm.org/managingsmart/articles/winter02/0102a.asp.

Notes and Responses to Case Questions:

Image © Jyothi Joshi, 2009. Used under license from Shutterstock.com

Tyler The Overnight Houseman

Case Type:	Issue Case
Main Subjects:	Coaching, Productivity
Who's Who:	• Shakia Andrews, *Executive Housekeeper*
	• Tyler O'Grady, *Overnight Houseman*

This evening Shakia had to stay late to help with the turndown service, and so she decided to wait until the overnight housemen arrived. Depending on the hotel occupation, two or three employees were scheduled. Overnight housemen were in charge of the Royal Hotel's complimentary shoeshine service. Shakia was chatting a little bit with the employees and opted to observe them while they were polishing shoes.

Tonight one of housemen was Tyler. He had been at the Royal Hotel for over a year, and no complaint had ever been received about his performance. Tyler was dependable and meticulous, but very, very slow.

Shakia watched as Tyler unhurriedly removed the laces to get access to the tongue of the shoe to prevent staining the laces. He then applied the polish to the shoe in slow, circular movements to ensure that the polish reached the inside of the creases. At the end, he meticulously, at a snail's pace, buffed the shoe until all traces of dullness had disappeared and the shoe shined to perfection.

Shakia admired his thoroughness, but Tyler took twice as long as the other housemen. Shakia was wondering, how she could quicken his pace?

The overnight houseman's job description included the following job requirements:

Perform routine work or the same task over and over again.

This person must have the ability to lift, pull, and push a moderate amount of weight.

This is a fast-paced position that will involve occasional customer interaction.

---

1. Describe the problem behavior.

2. What could be causing this behavior?

3. Highlight some of the consequences that the problem behavior has on others.

4. Outline some techniques supervisors could use to deal with the issue.

References

This case is inspired by a situation described in:

Albright, M., & Carr, C. (2002). *Solving on-the Job People Problems* (pp. 151–154). Paramus, NJ: Prentice Hall.

Notes and Responses to Case Questions:

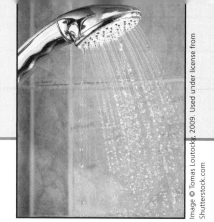

Case 23

Gentle Hints

Case Type:	**Incident Case**
Main Subjects:	**ADA, Coaching**
Who's Who:	• Jean Andres, *Front Desk Agent*
	• Dan Mazur, *Director of Rooms*
	• Allen Winston, *Regular Hotel Guest*

U pon checkout, Mr. Winston, one of the regular guests, approached Dan in the lobby. "Listen Dan, I had a great stay, but I need to share something with you. Jean, your front desk agent is an excellent employee, and I appreciate all that he does, but unfortunately he has a slight hygiene problem. Hmm, I wanted to tell you last month. It's his body odor and bad breath, I guess," said Mr. Winston slightly embarrassed. "You may want to give him some gentle hints," continued the guest. "Otherwise I will say 'Hi Jean' instead of 'Hello' next time I'm back," smiled Mr. Winston and walked to his car.

Dan returned to his office and was wondering how he should deal tactfully with this sensitive issue.

1. Identify potential reasons for the situation.

2. Highlight and evaluate possible actions Dan could take.

3. Who should deal with hygiene problems when they arise?

Notes and Responses to Case Questions:

The Slacker

Case Type:	Issue Case
Main Subjects:	Job Design/Job Description, Productivity, Work Systems
Who's Who:	• Jennifer Ortiz, *Restaurant Manager*
	• Tim Campbell, *Server Assistant*

Every time Jennifer came to the restaurant, she had the impression that Tim, one of the server assistants, was "goofing off." Even when the restaurant was packed, he was typically standing in a corner waiting to complete the next service step.

Server assistants have been assigned to work with a certain number of servers. They were rarely helping each other. Server assistants received a portion of the tip from their respective servers.

For managers, it was most frustrating to see his slow-moving motion while host persons and managers had to reset tables all the time. Jennifer barely had time to interact with guests and deal with other issues. Every time Tim was asked to help clear or reset tables in others sections, he claimed that he was busy with his own tables.

According to the notes of assistant managers, Tim was already advised to pull his own weight. Tim believed that he was doing his job as outlined in his job breakdown.

Jennifer knew that Tim and other server assistants should be more productive. She was rather desperate as she was reviewing the task breakdown. Some of the people around her did what they had to do, but nothing more.

Selected service steps as outlined in the Royal Standard Operation Procedures:

Task Breakdown	Steps	Responsibility	Timing Standard
1.	Greet guest at the door	Host/hostess	
2.	Escort and seat guest	Host/hostess	Within 2 minutes of arrival
3.	Explain the menu, take beverage order	Server	
4.	Serve bread and butter	Server assistant	Within 2 minutes of being seated
5.	Serve beverages	Server	Within 6 minutes of order taken
6.	Take food order	Server	
7.	Serve food items	Server	Within 15 minutes of order taken
8.	Clear table	Server assistant	Within 3 minutes of all guests' finishing
9.	Serve dessert	Server	
10.	Serve coffee	Server	
11.	Place check	Server	
12.	Reset table	Server assistant	Within 4 minutes of guests' departure

1. What seems to be happening in the restaurant? Describe the problem behavior.
2. What could be causing this behavior?
3. What recommendation might you have to improve the system? What further actions could Jennifer take in this situation?

Notes and Responses to Case Questions:

Case 25

Yasmine's Appraisal

Case Type:	**Application Case**
Main Subjects:	**Coaching, Feedback, Performance Appraisal**
Who's Who:	• Matthew Knorr, *Director of Food and Beverage*
	• Yasmine Lewis, *Hostess*
	• Jennifer Ortiz, *Restaurant Manager*

Jennifer glanced at her decorative wall calendar containing images of the local harvest festival. "It's already September. I should really sit down with Yasmine and do her yearly appraisal," she sighed.

The breakfast rush was over, and in addition the weekly Food and Beverage meeting got cancelled because Matthew, the F&B director, was still on vacation. So, Jennifer called the assistant manager on duty to cover the door for Yasmine while she is being reviewed for her annual appraisal. Jennifer printed the document and decided to quickly read it while waiting for Yasmine.

EXHIBITS

EXHIBIT 25.1

Royal Hotel—Manager's Handbook (Excerpts)

WRITING EMPLOYEE PERFORMANCE APPRAISALS—GUIDELINES

- When you evaluate an employee's performance, you need to consider behavior and results that you have observed and/or measured. You then need to decide whether the person's performance met, failed to meet, or exceeded expectations.
- It is the conclusions you draw from the facts that should lead to specific decisions and actions. The documents you write must not only communicate your conclusions, but they must include the details that clearly support those conclusions.
- A description is useful only if the details it includes are specific and complete. Instead of relying on subjective terms and vague statements that can be misunderstood, use objective language that describes observations.
- Acceptable performance documentation tells employees clearly what they are doing well and what they need to improve.
- Performance appraisals are to be completed in a timely manner.

EXHIBIT 25.2

THE ROYAL HOTEL
EMPLOYEE PERFORMANCE APPRAISAL

Name: Yasmine Lewis   **Department:** Harvest Room Restaurant

Job Title: Hostess   **Date In Position:** 7/1/2007

Appraisal Period: From 7/1/2007 To 6/30/2008

Appraisal Prepared By: **Date Appraisal Given:** 9/2/08
Jennifer Ortiz, Restaurant Manager

Next Level Approval: Date: ___/___/___

Evaluator Signature: Date: ___/___/___

Employee Signature: Date: ___/___/___

My signature acknowledges that this performance summary has been discussed with me.

1. LEVELS OF PERFORMANCE

Exceeds Standards   Performance and results achieved consistently exceed the standards and expectations for the position requirements.

Meets Standards   Performance and results achieved generally meet the standards and expectations for the position requirements.

Below Standards   Performance and results achieved consistently do not meet the standards and expectations for the position requirements.

2. SITUATION OVERVIEW

- The Harvest Room is one of the Royal Hotel's highest revenue generating outlets and is considered one of the top restaurants in the city.
- Yasmine transferred from the Stewarding Department to the Harvest Room in July 2007.
- She has come a long way from where she started. Yasmine was "thrown in" right in the thick of the busy season as the opening hostess.

3. PERFORMANCE FACTORS

ES = Exceeds Standards   MS = Meets Standards   BS = Below Standards

	ES	MS	BS
JOB KNOWLEDGE AND COMPREHENSION	ES		

JOB KNOWLEDGE AND COMPREHENSION
- She is very professional.
- Yasmine is a quick learner. She has been a guiding light when it comes to the training of other hosts/hostesses.

(continues)

EXHIBIT 25.2 (CONTINUED)

WORK QUALITY | | |BS|

- Yasmine does not complete the reservation book adequately.
- In addition she is often forgetful.
- Yasmine does not like answering the reservation hot line.
- More passion for perfection is needed.

PRODUCTIVITY/WORK HABITS |ES| | |

- She is very organized in regard to the upkeep of the Host stand.
- Yasmine is a team player.
- Yasmine knows her limitations; she is very vocal when it comes time for management assistance.

GROOMING |ES| | |

- Yasmine exhibits appropriate grooming; she is better dressed than the other AM hostess.

INITIATIVE/PROBLEM SOLVING | |MS| |

- Although this area has yet to truly be tested, Yasmine should focus on quickly resolving issues that may arise and learn to properly use her resources to multitask.

INTERPERSONAL SKILLS | |MS| |

- Unfortunately, she received numerous complaints regarding her attitude.
- Although she is a nice person, she doesn't take criticism well. She has a tendency to be condescending when interacting with management.

This is something we would like Yasmine to take note and improve on.

CUSTOMER RELATIONS |ES| | |

- Yasmine is good with Royal customers.

ATTENDANCE AND PUNCTUALITY | | |BS|

- Yasmine incurred a high number of incidents of tardiness over the last 12 months.
- We expect better attendance.
- She did not show up for work on Sunday, 6/29/2008.

TOTAL | |MS| |

4. OVERALL RATING

To conclude, Yasmine is one of the key players of the Harvest Room and a valuable part of the Royal Hotel. She has been climbing up hill since she started, and she will continue to learn as time goes by. Yasmine has become settled in her position.

(continues)

EXHIBIT 25.2 (CONTINUED)

5. RECOMMENDATIONS FOR FUTURE DEVELOPMENT

- Fine-tuning the service quality and becoming more knowledgeable will broaden her radar and eye for detail.
- She needs to be "warm and fuzzy" with others.

Yasmine, you recently expressed interest in becoming a supervisor. You are on the right track! Keep it up and you may get a promotion sooner than you think.

6. EMPLOYEE COMMENTS AND SIGNATURE:

---

1. Let's help Jennifer. Read through the performance documentation (Exhibits 25.1 and 25.2). What mistakes did she make? Use your imagination and revise the statements where appropriate.

2. How should managers keep track of employees' performance?

3. Should Jennifer go over the employee's appraisal with her manager before she reviews it with Yasmine?

References

Chan, J. F., & Lutovich, D. (1994). *Writing Performance Documentation: A Self-Paced Training Program.* San Anselmo, CA: Advanced Communication Designs, Inc.

Falcone, P. (1999). Rejuvenate your performance evaluation writing skills. *HRMagazine, 44*(10), 126–136.

Society of Human Resource Management. (1996, March). *Performance Appraisals: A Collection of Samples,* 2nd ed. Alexandria, VA: SHRM.

Notes and Responses to Case Questions:

PART FOUR

Encouraging
Others

Case 26

I Am Just a Part-Timer

Case Type:	Issue Case
Main Subjects:	Coaching, Motivation, Rewards, Work Systems
Who's Who:	• Betty Chu, *Human Resources Manager*
	• Leslie Rudick, *Candidate*

Betty, from Human Resources called Leslie this morning. "I am delighted to inform you that we can offer you now a part-time position at the front desk."

"Great," answered Leslie, "I've finished my midterms, I can't wait to start this weekend job."

"Alright, the next step for you is to attend our two-day orientation on Monday and Tuesday next week," explained Betty.

"Oops," answered Leslie, "I have classes on both these days and I cannot miss more classes."

"You know Leslie, without completing the orientation you may not be employed in this hotel. Would you like to call me back?" Betty said.

For Leslie, this front desk position was only a stopover in her pursuit of a career elsewhere. But she considered herself a hard-working and productive individual. Leslie, had various short-term positions in the past, and Betty's call provoked the usual feeling of being a temporary worker who is easily replaceable.

1. What are the advantages of using part-time employees?

2. Consider ways of hiring that can help the Royal Hotel lengthen the part-time relationship.

3. What recommendations would you give to Royal management in terms of offering training for part-timers in more creative ways?

4. Most part-timers do not intend to stay with one employer for years. How can management maximize the value of the time part-timers spend with Royal Hotel?

Notes and Responses to Case Questions:

Image © franck camhl, 2009. Used under license from Shutterstock.com

Housekeeping
Guest Satisfaction Scores

Case Type:	**Head Case**
Main Subjects:	**Motivation, Rewards**
Who's Who:	• Shakia Andrews, *Executive Housekeeper*

S hakia was desperate. The guest satisfaction scores for the Housekeeping department have been extremely low for the past year. Though the Housekeeping management has been in place for several years, nearly all of the guestroom attendants have been employed by the Royal Hotel for less than two years. Shakia was not sure what had caused the perceived level of service and cleanliness to suffer.

1. Why are the guest service scores for the Housekeeping department usually low?

2. Housekeeping managers often realize that probably the hardest part of their job is to motivate their staff. Explain.

3. Where should Shakia begin to raise the guest satisfactions scores?

4. To maintain the commitment of housekeepers, identify creative intrinsic[1] and extrinsic[2] rewards.

Notes

[1]**Intrinsic rewards** are received by the individual directly through task performance. (Satisfactions derived from the job itself, such as pride in one's work, a feeling of accomplishment, or being part of a team.)

[2]**Extrinsic rewards** are external to the job and provided by the employer. (Benefits provided by the employer, usually money, promotion, or other benefits.)

Reference

Frye, W. D. (2007, July/August). Determining why housekeeping guest service scores are low. *The Rooms Chronicle, 5.*

Notes and Responses to Case Questions:

The Dead-Ender

Case Type:	Issue Case
Main Subjects:	Motivation, Organizational Structure, Promotion, Rewards
Who's Who:	• Carlos Diaz, *Guest Services Manager*
	• Amy Polak, *Assistant Front Office Manager*
	• Marina Wright, *Revenue Manager*

Amy felt that she has stayed in the same job for too long, far longer than originally promised.

She joined the Royal Hotel as an assistant front office manager four years ago. She enjoyed her job, many of the front desk agents who worked under her wings had become "Employee of the Month." Lately she was wondering why she was never considered for the "Manager of the Quarter" award.

Her problem was that while she was always busy, she wasn't learning anything new. She'd seen all the issues before. Besides boredom or the sense that everything was too repetitive, she felt that she has been taken for granted.

What has driven Amy is her desire to become a hotel manager. Both of the past two Directors of Rooms said they were satisfied with her performance but explained to her that Rooms Division had no prospects for promotion in the near future. She remembered that Marina and Carlos also had started their careers at the front desk and now they are both department heads. Amy felt that career opportunities have become limited for her … the career ladder is blocked. She loved the Royal Hotel, but in the last one or two years she's found herself thinking about leaving.

1. What are some of the reasons for employees' dissatisfaction when reaching a stage where growth or movement has stopped?

2. What are some of the benefits of being temporarily plateaued?

3. What may be some of the negative effects of plateauing on the person and organization?

4. Individuals often become "indispensable" and are prevented from promotions. What are the consequences of this practice?

5. What are some techniques to motivate employees in the absence of promotion opportunities?

Reference

Bardwick, J. M. (1986). *The Plateauing Trap: How to Avoid It in Your Career ... Your Life.* New York: Amacom.

Notes and Responses to Case Questions:

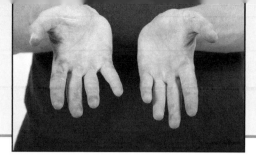

Image © Lucian Coman, 2009. Used under license
from Shutterstock.com

Tainted Occupations

Case Type:	Issue Case
Main Subjects:	Job Design/Job Description, Motivation
Who's Who:	• Matthew Knorr, *Director of Food and Beverage*
	• Merrick Lew, *Assistant Chief Steward*

Merrick recently graduated from a prestigious hospitality program. His dream has always been to become a Food and Beverage director. The Royal Hotel offered him the assistant chief steward position. Originally Merrick was hoping to start in a customer contact position, but Matthew convinced him that this job will help him to achieve his career goals.

When he accepted the position, he immediately called his parents to share the news. His dad was impressed by the title. He asked Merrick what the position exactly consisted of.

"Actually, I will be in charge of the hotel's china/glass/silver budget," answered Merrick. He felt slightly embarrassed and did not say that actually he will be the boss of the dishwashers.

1. Dirty work refers to occupations that are viewed by society as physically, socially, or morally tainted. Most dirty work occupations appear to have relatively low prestige (i.e., function of status, power, education, income). Please provide a few examples for dirty occupations in the hotel industry.

2. What challenges do managers in dirty work occupations face?

3. What tactics can a manager use to neutralize the attributes of the work that render it seemingly dirty?

4. How can management enhance occupational dignity and esteem in dirty work positions?

Notes and Responses to Case Questions:

The GM's Morning Round

Case Type:	**Application Case**
Main Subjects:	**Feedback, Motivation, Organizational Politics, Respect**
Who's Who:	• Shakia Andrews, *Executive Housekeeper*
	• Lori Canelle, *Spa Manager*
	• Evelyn Collins, *Room Service Assistant Manager*
	• Carlos Diaz, *Guest Services Manager*
	• Brooke Garofalo, *Front Desk Agent*
	• Jarrett Geller, *Hotel Guest, Conference Organizer*
	• Evan Grafton, *Valet Parker*
	• Amber Kerkorian, *Spa Supervisor*
	• Robert Kunz, *General Manager*
	• Jason Lim, *Front Desk Agent*
	• Debbie Murphy, *Sales Manager*
	• Fiona O'Brien, *Public Relations Manager*
	• Kristen Palmer, *Regular Restaurant Guest*
	• Jane Peterson, *Hotel Manager*
	• Zachary Savin, *Restaurant Server*
	• Sabrina Schmidt, *Bartender*
	• Dylan Shaw, *Bartender*
	• David Steele, *Security Manager*
	• Hailey Valletta, *Assistant Revenue Manager*

The Royal's executive committee invited a famous motivational speaker to the last management retreat. Robert Kunz spent the entire weekend reviewing the handout they were given. He learned a lot about positive reinforcement and other morale-boosting strategies that can work at the Royal Hotel. Monday morning he decided to get out of the executive office suite to engage hotel employees at all levels.

Stop 1—Sales

He decided to begin his round at the Sales department. "Good morning Mr. Kunz," Debbie, the Sales manager, greeted him. "Hello, Debbie, I am so happy that I bumped into you," Mr. Kunz told her. "I need to tell you that you do an amazing job with our clients; keep up the good work," the GM smiled and proceeded to the restaurant to have a coffee.

Stop 2—Restaurant

"I'm sure this is the day Mr. Kunz will say something!" Zachary, one of the servers, murmured to himself. The other day, Ms. Palmer, one of the regular guests, mentioned to Zachary that she had sent a letter to Mr. Kunz a month ago. Ms. Palmer mentioned that she had specifically asked Mr. Kunz to praise his outstanding performance. Zachary was first uncomfortable with what Ms. Palmer had done, but at the same time he was excited about the possibility of being personally recognized by Mr. Kunz.

As usual, Mr. Kunz was happy with Zachary's service. He finished his cappuccino, signed the check, and left the restaurant. "See you Mr. Kunz … maybe tomorrow," Zachary told him and started to clean the table.

Stop 3—Reservation

After his coffee, he briefly visited the Reservation office. Hailey, the assistant manager, was about to finalize the 10-day forecast. "I've come to personally congratulate you Hailey for your accurate forecasts. What would I do without you?" Mr. Kunz told her, while studying the printout and slowly walking down the corridor between the cubicles.

Stop 4—Front Desk

"Good morning Brooke. I heard so much about you! Mr. Geller, who organized the two-day pharmaceutical conference this week, couldn't stop mentioning your name." Mr. Kunz greeted one of the Front Desk agents. Brooke felt very good about Mr. Kunz's kind approach. She already knew that using names can personalize interactions. It's a little thing, but it works.

At the same time she felt somewhat confused about the situation. She was off the last two days and she'd never met Mr. Geller. As soon as Jason, the other Front Desk agent finished a guest checkout, she walked over to him and proudly said, "You know, Mr. Kunz knows my name."

"Yes, he asked me two minutes ago, what the name of the other Front Desk agent was." Jason said. "By the way, I authorized a late checkout to Mr. Geller in room #325. He is the nicest guest I've ever had," he added and acknowledged the next guest in line.

Stop 5—Guest Services

Evan, a long-time employee, was the valet parker this morning. Mr. Kunz approached him with uncontrollable enthusiasm. "Absolutely super; that was really great how you pulled this expensive car. We are all very impressed. Well done."

Carlos overheard the conversation and looked puzzled. He wanted to sit down this morning with Evan and have a serious heart-to-heart with him. Evan was a pleasant person but did only the minimum, the kind of person who never deviates from the book.

Stop 6—Housekeeping

Mr. Kunz liked to stop by Housekeeping, because he believed that those employees deserve daily stimulation. Shakia had just started the pre-shift briefing when he arrived. Housekeepers were informed on what was going on at the Royal, including who's checking in so that everyone was on the same page. To lift employee spirit, Kunz provided kudos to all employees by saying that he'd always dreamed of managing an "all-star team" and gave everyone a pin for uniforms that says "Bravo." At the end of the meeting he took a photo of the entire staff wearing the new pin. It will be great for the bulletin board. For his next Housekeeping visit, Mr. Kunz has just signed a rush order this morning for T-shirts that say "Pat on the back."

Stop 7—Room Service

Evelyn, one of the A.M. assistant managers in Room Service, was inspecting an order when Mr. Kunz arrived. The hotel was fully booked last night, and Kunz heard from Jane earlier that Evelyn asked for help. "Well done! You handled the crunch situation this morning very effectively," the general manager told her. "It's too bad, that even with extra assistance hotel corridors are full of dirty room service carts," added Mr. Kunz.

Stop 8—SPA

He continued his tour at the spa. At 9:30 A.M. Jane paged Kunz and informed him that Lori called in sick and she thinks that Amber, the morning supervisor, should stay longer because many VIP guests have made massage appointments.

The general manager approached Amber, who was serving fresh lemonade to guests.

"I can't tell you, Amber, how much we appreciate how you help us maintain our high service standards." He started the conversation with her.

"It's my job," she answered pleasantly. Amber was astonished because she had never received any kind of compliment regarding her performance here at Royal.

"By the way," smiled Mr. Kunz. "Would you be available to pick up an extra shift this afternoon?"

Stop 9—Lounge

Sabrina and Dylan, the two bartenders, were polishing martini glasses when Mr. Kunz showed up. "Here is our 'top mixologist.' How proud we are of you," shouted Kunz and pointed toward Sabrina. One of the local magazines published a "Beloved Bartender" section every three years. They named the top bartenders in the city, did a little profile on them, and listed their favorite cocktail recipes. A journalist contacted Fiona a few months ago, and they decided together that Sabrina should be featured in the magazine.

"You see Dylan, you should be more like Sabrina," turned Kunz to the other bartender.

Stop 10—Security

The GM concluded his morning round in the small Security office. He came to praise David for his professionalism during the power outage a day before.

Mr. Kunz had a firm handshake. David noticed that when Mr. Kunz shook his hand he used his other hand covering the shake and held his hand for longer than normal. Mr. Kunz asked David to remain seated. He was standing with hands on hips, elbows out to the sides. David felt slightly uncomfortable because the general manager took up lots up of space. Also, Mr. Kunz placed his hand twice on his arm during conversation and interrupted him a few times.

1. Evaluate the manager's effectiveness in motivating his employees in each situation as follows.
   a. What key mistakes is Mr. Kunz making?
   b. Describe the effect of his approach on employees.
   c. What suggestions would you make to Mr. Kunz?

2. Do we need praise every time employees do a good job?

3. Employees don't always react to praise in a gracious way. Why?

4. Telling employees "you're doing a great job" isn't specific enough. Develop a list of "openers" that you can use to keep praise specific.

Notes and Responses to Case Questions:

The Chef's
Incentive Program

Case Type:	**Data Case**
Main Subjects:	**Controlling Costs, Motivation, Rewards**
Who's Who:	• Pascal Gateau, *Executive Chef*
	• Matthew Knorr, *Director of Food and Beverage*
	• Robert Kunz, *General Manager*
	• Jane Peterson, *Hotel Manager*

The executive committee meeting was short today. Mr. Kunz asked everyone to further cut costs and then abruptly left the meeting room. Jane looked at Matthew and asked him while smiling, "So, how could Food and Beverage contribute to the welfare of the Royal Hotel?"

Matthew looked at the next year's F&B budget and sighed.

"You'll need to institute an aggressive incentive program based on food cost saving for the chef," continued Jane.

"Should I give him a substantial bonus if he reaches our goal?" asked Matthew.

"My suggestion is that instead of a single goal level with the bonus being 'all or nothing,' you should create multiple goal levels with a different bonus level attached to each—basically the higher the goal level attained, the higher the reward," Jane concluded.

1. Describe the disadvantages of individual monetary incentives.

2. What are the advantages of creating multiple goal levels with a different bonus level attached to each?

3. To achieve a food cost percentage below budget, develop an individual incentive program for the chef. Assuming that the food revenue budget is maintained, determine the award values based on improvement. (Ten percent of the saving is typically a good benchmark.)

4. Write a brief memorandum to the chef outlining the program. Make sure that the chef sees a clear link between his efforts and the incentive payout.

5. What are the pitfalls associated with incentives based solely on cost control? How could Matthew improve the chef's incentive program?

Additional Information

Budgeted yearly food revenue: $2,000,000

Budgeted food cost: 25.5%

Reference

Locke, E. A. (2004). Linking goals to monetary incentives. *Academy of Management Executive, 18*(4), 130–133.

Notes and Responses to Case Questions:

Dealing with Problem Behaviors

Introduction

Culture Promotes Behavioral Norms

Company culture describes the company, how it is managed, how it reacts to external challenges and how workers respond to their work environment. Company culture can be divided into three general categories: Constructive, Passive/Defensive and Aggressive/Defensive (Cooke & Szumal and Human Synergistics International).

The Constructive culture is the most desirable and the least found. It is typified by the following norms:

- Achievement
- Self-Actualizing
- Humanistic–Encouraging
- Affiliative

Passive/Defensive cultures are characterized by the following norms:

- Approval
- Conventional
- Dependent
- Avoidance

Aggressive/Defensive cultures are encompassing the following norms:

- Oppositional
- Power

- Competitive
- Perfectionistic

Inappropriate Behaviors in the Workplace

Human behavior is shaped by various factors and organizational members may not always behave in ways consistent with their company's prevailing culture.

However, it is obvious that defensive cultural norms (both passive and aggressive) will negatively impact employees' behavior.

In this chapter we will present all sorts of difficult employees—more often to be encountered in organizations with nonconstructive cultures. Each difficult person and his or her particular form of difficult behavior present a unique challenge for the management. Unfortunately, no one has the perfect solution for handling such people; at the same time, if we look for patterns of behavior, we can prepare ourselves for dealing with them.

References

Cooke, R. A., & Szumal, J. L. (2000). Using the organizational culture Inventory to understand the operating cultures of organizations. In N. M. Ashkanasy, C. P. M. Wilderom, & M. F. Peterson (Eds.) (2000). Handbook of organizational culture and climate (pp. 147–162). Thousand Oaks, CA: Sage Publications, Inc.

Human Synergistics International. (n.d.) Introducing the circumplex. Retrieved July 14, 2007, from http://www.humansynergistics.com/system/default.aspx

Circumplex style and cluster names from Robert A. Cooke and J. Clayton Lafferty, Organizational Culture Inventory®, Human Synergistics International. Copyright © 1987–2009. All rights reserved. Used by permission.

Behaviors Promoted by Passive/Defensive Cultures

Case 32

Peter Is the Nicest Manager!

Case Type:	Issue Case
Main Subjects:	Coaching, Feedback, Self-Confidence, Trust
Who's Who:	• Judith Grace, *Front Office Manager*
	• Peter Klema, Assistant Front Office Manager

Judith called Peter, one of the assistant Front Office managers, to her office. "What can I do for you?" Peter asked with a big smile on his face. Judith felt very comfortable with Peter. Peter was a long-term employee and always had a friendly word for everyone. He was one of those employees who never said "NO."

"This is regarding the new Shift Checklists." Judith started the conversation. "I e-mailed you the proposal a while ago," she continued. "Do you have any thoughts; anything that you didn't like about it?"

"It's great!" said Peter.

"Hmmm, alright, in this case, could you make sure it is implemented as soon as possible?" Judith asked. "As you know Peter, I will be on vacation for the next two weeks and I count on you."

"No problem Judith. It will be introduced next week." Peter said and as he was leaving the office jokingly added, "It's always a pleasure doing business with you Judith."

When Judith got back from vacation, she noticed that the staff was still using the old Shift Checklists, which did not include important new procedures to be completed.

1. Describe the problem behavior.

2. Identify potential reasons for the difficult behavior.

3. Highlight some of the consequences that the problem behavior has on others.

4. How would you handle the situation now?

5. Outline some techniques Judith should have used in the first place to handle the situation.

Notes and Responses to Case Questions:

Case 33

The "Invisible" Accounting Clerk

Case Type:	Head Case
Main Subjects:	Coaching, Feedback, Rapport, Self-Confidence
Who's Who:	• Mike Lee, *Accounting Manager*
	• Jack Aggott, *Accounts Receivable Clerk*

Mike Lee, the Accounting manager, sighed as Jack was leaving his office. He had a very hard time communicating with Jack. Jack was shy and kept a low profile, but what bothered Mike the most was that every time he asked him a question, all he was getting in response was a "yep" or a "nope." He did not sense any negativity or calculated aggression in this behavior. Jack joined the Royal Hotel nine months ago as an Accounts Receivable clerk. He is responsible for processing billing for hotel guests and functions. Mike also noticed in the weekly accounting meetings that Jack never had anything to contribute. Jack was almost an "invisible" character of the hotel. Mike was wondering who signed off on Jack's probationary review three months ago without making any comments on Jack's communication skills. Mike was wondering how to deal with Jack.

1. Describe the problem behavior.
2. Identify potential reasons for the difficult behavior. Why do so many people describe themselves as shy?
3. What are some of the negative consequences of shyness in the workplace?
4. How would you increase shy employees' comfort level?

Notes and Responses to Case Questions:

Case 34

The Wishy-Washy Manager

Case Type:	Issue Case
Main Subjects:	Coaching, Decision Making, Feedback
Who's Who:	• Matthew Knorr, *Director of Food and Beverage*
	• Emily Perkins, *Lounge and Bar Manager*

After the Food and Beverage meeting Matthew asked Emily to stay back for a minute and asked her, "Emily, have you made up your mind? Do you think we should increase the bar par stock level? We discussed this last month."

"Do I have to decide now? What do you think I should do?" Emily replied.

"Well, you are the bar manager. . ." insisted Matthew.

"Why don't you decide on this Matthew? I promise I'll go with the flow," answered Emily, with a charming facial expression. At this point Matthew was paged and had to leave the meeting room.

1. Describe the problem behavior.

2. Identify potential reasons for the difficult behavior.

3. Highlight some of consequences that the problem behavior has on the operation.

4. If you were Matthew, how would you handle the situation?

Notes and Responses to Case Questions:

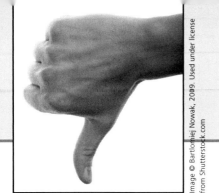

Case 35

I Was
Just Kidding!

Case Type:	Head Case
Main Subjects:	Feedback, Humor/Sarcasm, Incivility, Meetings, Respect
Who's Who:	• Carlos Diaz, *Guest Services Manager*
	• Dan Mazur, *Director of Rooms*
	• Kalinda Stenton, *PBX Manager*

arlos Diaz raised his hand during divisional meeting. "Go ahead, Carlos" Dan said.

"Actually, I put together a citywide valet parking price comparison." Carlos told him.

"Wow, did you do this all by yourself?" asked Kalinda and turned her thumb down laughingly. Some started to laugh. Carlos laughed with the others, but he also felt bad about the situation. Kalinda was a good colleague, who had finished her first year as PBX manager, but it was obvious that she wanted to move to a position with increased responsibility soon.

As he looked at Kalinda, she quickly mumbled to him, "I was just kidding." Carlos didn't think that Dan could hear Kalinda's sarcastic comment because he was briefly answering a phone call. Carlos was wondering how he should follow up on this.

1. Describe the problem behavior.

2. Identify potential reasons for the difficult behavior.

3. Highlight some of the consequences that the problem behavior has on others.

4. Outline some techniques supervisors could use to deal with the issue.

Notes and Responses to Case Questions:

Did You Hear What Lori Did Last Night?

Case Type:	**Incident Case**
Main Subject:	**Feedback, Gossip**
Who's Who:	• Lori Canelle, *Spa Manager*
	• Yvonne Clark, *Director of Sales and Marketing*
	• Debbie Murphy, *Sales Manager*
	• Brian White, *Assistant Director of Engineering*

It was a hot day in July. After the sales meeting, Yvonne and Debbie stayed back for small talk around the water cooler. Debbie smiled and asked Yvonne, "Did you hear what Lori did last night?"

"I am sure you will tell me. What would I do without you? How else would I know what is really happening in this hotel?" answered Yvonne.

"Well, I heard from a good source that Lori and Brian, you know the guy from Engineering, . . ." Debbie went on with her story, with some juicy details.

1. Describe the problem behavior.

2. Identify potential reasons for the difficult behavior.

3. Highlight some of the consequences that the problem behavior has on others.

4. Describe the communication failure that occurred in this case.

5. Outline some techniques Yvonne should have used to deal with this specific issue.

6. How can managers further combat this problem and minimize gossips' damaging effects?

Notes and Responses to Case Questions:

Case 37

The Weak Link

Case Type:	**Incident Case**
Main Subjects:	**Authority, Organizational Politics, Organizational Structure, Recruiting/Selection, Team Building**
Who's Who:	• Pascal Gateau, *Executive Chef*
	• Matthew Knorr, *Director of Food and Beverage*
	• Jennifer Ortiz, *Restaurant Manager*

"Service was really subpar today," Chef Gateau told Matthew after dinner service. Jennifer walked in to the chef's office and overheard him.

"Chef, could you share a little glory with the front of house please?" Jennifer asked.

"There is no secret here Jennifer. All I want is to get another diamond for the restaurant," chef replied.

"I know chef. We discussed it a couple of times," Jennifer said and walked away.

The next day, Jennifer went to see Matthew to talk to him about what is going on between the two departments. She quoted the chef saying, "The main stumbling block to restaurant nirvana is the front of house." Jennifer explained to Matthew how much she admires and respects the chef but, at the same time, she has the feeling that the service is blamed for all errors, as if a 45-minute wait for entrées was the server's fault. Matthew promised her that he would deal with the situation.

1. Describe the problem behavior.

2. Identify potential reasons for the difficult behavior.

3. Highlight some of the consequences that the problem behavior has on others.

4. How do you think Matthew should deal with the chef?

5. Outline some techniques supervisors could use to deal with blaming in general.

6. It is important not hire blamers in the first place. Recommend a good interview question to avoid hiring a "blamer."

Reference
Bonadies, M. (2004, June). I've got nothing against chefs. *Santé*, 20.

Notes and Responses to Case Questions:

Behaviors Promoted by Aggressive/ Defensive Cultures

Case 38

It Won't Work!

Case Type:	Issue Case
Main Subjects:	Change, Coaching, Feedback, Meetings
Who's Who:	• Bruce Baber, *Assistant Catering Manager*
	• Laura Coe, *Assistant Catering Manager*
	• Petra Wolf, *Assistant Catering Manager*
	• Kelly Woodstock, *Catering Manager*

"I am sorry to tell you guys, but we are behind budget," Kelly said at the start of the catering meeting. "We all agree that the meetings market is lucrative. What techniques do you think we should use to reach those folks?" she asked and looked at the three catering assistant managers, Bruce, Laura, and Petra.

Both Petra and Laura came up with some ideas. Petra suggested that a carefully planned sales blitz[1] may be the right technique. She energetically stood up and started to put some buzzwords on a flip chart on how she would organize it. "Last month, we identified 500 prospects that qualify as new business. I suggest that we should do a three-day sales blitz and. . .," Petra explained.

Bruce interrupted her, "Yeah, and who would do it?"

Petra was ready with the answer, "Spring break is coming up in four weeks. Let's hire some sales-oriented college students from the local hospitality program to reinforce our team."

Bruce cut Petra off again, "We tried that couple of years ago. It's intrusive and won't work. Let's move on."

Petra wanted to explain that it would not be an unannounced cold call—the prospective clients would be advised ahead of time, but she changed her mind and sat down.

Kelly looked puzzled and asked if anyone would like to continue the discussion with some other ideas. No one responded, so Kelly moved to the next point on the agenda.

Laura, the junior catering manager who originally wanted to present her plan, slowly put her paperwork away. It was not the first time that Bruce shot down ideas. Laura joined the Royal Hotel last year; during her interview, Kelly made her believe that creativity and innovation are important for the hotel. She now felt disappointed.

1. Describe the problem behavior.
2. Identify potential reasons for the difficult behavior.
3. Highlight some of the consequences that the problem behavior has on others.
4. Describe the communication failure that occurred in this case.
5. Outline some techniques managers could use to deal with negative people.

Note
[1]SALES BLITZ
A sales blitz focuses on contacting potential clients in a concentrated area over a brief period of time.

Notes and Responses to Case Questions:

Image © Le Loft 1911, 2009. Used under license from Shutterstock.com

Case 39

That's Just
How the Chef Is!

Case Type: Issue Case

Main Subjects: Bullying, Chain of Command, Coaching, Feedback, Harassment, Incivility, Performance Appraisal, Self-Confidence

Who's Who:
- Pascal Gateau, *Executive Chef*
- Matthew Knorr, *Director of Food and Beverage*
- Katherine Norton, *Director of Human Resources*

Matthew was troubled by the results of the quarterly turnover and exit interview summary. According to the document, five kitchen employees resigned. Four employees claimed that the chef was the cause of their departure. Here are some comments employees made:

"The chef regularly loses his temper and verbally abuses us."

"Gateau is well known as tyrant. He yelled and screamed at us all the time."

"The chef took advantage of me and treated everyone like scum."

"He is always giving me dirty looks; he has unreasonable expectations."

"Why do you think so many people last only a few months?"

Surprisingly, one of the employees, who left for family reasons, spoke very highly about the executive chef: "I loved this place! I came to the Royal Hotel right after military school and Chef Gateau helped me a lot to become a team player and a good chef de partie. Advancement is based on individual ability and achievement. I will be back one day."

Matthew remembered that the other day, he stepped in the chef's office to check something with him regarding the menu; he told him that he would rather meet with him elsewhere because the kitchen is his territory.

Matthew knew that resigning employees exaggerate sometimes, but decided to briefly discuss the results with Katherine after the executive committee meeting. She carefully listened to Matthew and replied quietly, "That's just how the chef is."

1. Describe the problem behavior.
2. What is the difference between harassment and bullying?
3. Identify potential reasons for the difficult behavior. How does this behavior affect the work environment?
4. Highlight some consequences that the problem behavior has on others.
5. It seems that the chef can get away with his inappropriate behavior. Highlight some potential reasons.
6. Outline some techniques management could use to deal with the chef.
7. Could you identify two specific Human Resource techniques?
   a. Avoid hiring potential bullies.
   b. Suggest a performance appraisal technique to curtail workplace incivility.

Notes and Responses to Case Questions:

Case 40

The Expert

Case Type: Issue Case

Main Subjects: Authority, Coaching, Self-Confidence

Who's Who:
- Bob Biel, *Assistant Housekeeping Manager*
- Shakia Andrews, *Executive Housekeeper*
- Chloe Reilly, *Housekeeper*

Bob recently graduated from a prestigious hospitality program. He joined the Royal Hotel a year ago as an assistant housekeeping manager with the hope that he can become a department head after completing his first year. Bob was very dynamic and productive. He distinguished himself as a knowledgeable employee. At the same time, Shakia, his supervisor, often felt that Bob's management style was overbearing. The other day she overheard how Bob was giving feedback to a longtime housekeeper: "Chloe, that's not the right way to do that. I know better than you how to roll the pillows and the bedspread toward the headboard."

Bob constantly gave unwanted advice to everyone and knew everything. She also noticed that other assistant managers never socialized with Bob, and morale was down in the office.

The last incident occurred this morning when Shakia arrived. "How is everything Bob?" she asked as she entered the office.

"Good, Shakia. I told the housekeepers this morning not to use sanitizer when cleaning the bathroom floor; the all-purpose cleaner is more than enough."

"Bob, it is our standard to mop the floor with a sanitizer," Shakia replied.

"I thought that we need to save money," Bob said.

"Let's sit down this afternoon before you leave," Shakia answered.

1. Describe Bob's behavior.

2. Identify potential reasons for Bob's difficult behavior.

3. Highlight some of the consequences that the problem behavior has on others.

4. Outline some techniques Shakia should use to deal with Bob.

Notes and Responses to Case Questions:

Case 41

Jeff, You Test My Patience!

Case Type:	**Issue Case**
Main Subjects:	**Analytical, Big Picture, Coaching, Feedback**
Who's Who:	• Jeff Gillespie, *Assistant Banquet Manager*
	• Thomas Waxer, *Banquet Manager*

Thomas was surprised when Jeff, the new assistant banquet manager, arrived with a stack of professional books and "how-to guides." "Don't' worry Thomas, I'm not a perfectionist," Jeff told him. Thomas smiled, because he could not remember the last time he had five minutes to read a book in the office.

In the weekly event meetings Jeff was very attentive. At the same time, Thomas noticed that Jeff always recalculated forecasts and pricing estimates sent by catering. Jeff spent hours analyzing the banquet event orders and suggested the implementation of mathematical probability analysis to reduce the risk for underestimating the number of no-shows. This last idea tested Thomas's patience, and he stopped the project.

A few weeks ago when Jeff was in charge, a wedding guest was complaining that the buffet was not decorated well enough and the event overall was lacking creativity. Also, Jeff forgot to send the leftover cake to the bridal suite. Aside from this incident, Thomas was happy with Jeff, but sometimes he wondered if banquet management was the right job for Jeff.

1. Describe the problem behavior.

2. Identify potential reasons for the difficult behavior.

3. Highlight some of the consequences that the problem behavior has on others.

4. Outline some general techniques supervisors could use to deal with similar issues.

5. What should Thomas do?

Notes and Responses to Case Questions:

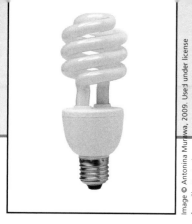

Image © Antonina Murawa, 2009. Used under license from Shutterstock.com

The Perfect Change of Lightbulbs

Case Type:	Issue Case
Main Subjects:	**Big Picture, Coaching, Perfectionism**
Who's Who:	• Charlie Jones, *Director of Engineering*
	• Katherine Norton, *Director of Human Resources*
	• Brian White, *Assistant Director of Engineering*

"Should we have lunch together?" Charlie suggested to his assistant Brian.

"Sure, I will join you in a second," Brian answered and started to straighten every stack on his desk before leaving the office.

Charlie was patiently waiting while Brian made sure that all books, pens, and folders were perfectly aligned. "Did you have a chance to send out the memo regarding energy saving techniques?" he asked Brian.

"I will do it first thing tomorrow morning. I just want to run a quick spell-check," explained Brian.

"I thought we reviewed the memo last week," Charlie interrupted.

Brian worked very hard and tried to go several steps beyond "going that extra mile." He recently launched a new engineering initiative. In this new program Brian is offering new techniques to employees on how to replace lightbulbs perfectly.

Katherine mentioned to Charlie the other day that one of the engineering employees was complaining in Human Resource about Brian. According to the employee, Brian is intolerant of even the slightest mistakes. He can dwell on errors for days, and most of the engineers work in constant fear of slipping up. As they were walking down to the cafeteria, Charlie was wondering what to tell his assistant.

1. Describe the problem behavior.

2. Identify potential reasons for the difficult behavior.

3. Highlight some of the consequences that the problem behavior has on others.

4. Outline some techniques Charlie could use to deal with the issue.

Reference

Raudsepp, E. (1990). Is perfectionism holding your career back? *Supervision, 51* (8), 3–5.

Notes and Responses to Case Questions:

Case 43

The "Bleeding Heart" of the Hotel

Case Type:	Issue Case
Main Subjects:	Coaching, Flexibility, Workaholism
Who's Who:	• Jennifer Ortiz, *Restaurant Manager*
	• Paul Yurkonis, *Assistant Restaurant Manager*

The restaurant was rather slow that day, and Jennifer was ready to leave. "Are you heading home soon too?" Jennifer asked Paul, one of the assistant managers.

"I have some paperwork to finish," answered Paul.

Jennifer was hesitating a moment and asked him, "Would you like me to stay and help you?"

"No, I will just do it by myself. Thanks anyway." Paul smiled and turned the computer on.

Paul had been at the Royal much longer than Jennifer and when she joined the hotel, she quickly realized that Paul is the "bleeding heart" of the hotel. He comes in early and leaves late—every single day. Jennifer noticed that Paul was even around on his days off. Paul was very dependable and willing, and still, he somehow made Jennifer feel that his great attitude was not appreciated. Flexibility and hard work was expected throughout the hotel, as stated in the manager's handbook:

"As a manager, you may be required to put in excess hours to complete assignments and projects related to your position."

Jennifer certainly valued Paul's efforts but she was concerned as well. She was unsure if she should address the situation.

1. Describe the problem behavior.

2. Identify potential reasons for the difficult behavior.

3. Highlight some of consequences that the problem behavior has on the operation.

4. Outline some techniques managers could use to deal in similar issues.

Notes and Responses to Case Questions:

TEAMWO R K

Breaking Down the Barriers

Case Type:	Issue Case
Main Subjects:	Organizational Structure, Team Building, Work Systems
Who's Who:	• Shakia Andrews, *Executive Housekeeper*
	• Judith Grace, *Front Office Manager*
	• Robert Kunz, *General Manager*
	• Dan Mazur, *Director of Rooms*
	• Jane Peterson, *Hotel Manager*

an was rather shocked as he was reviewing the results of the yearly employee survey.

Here are some of the issues highlighted by Front Office employees:

"There are excessive delays in getting rooms clean for arriving guests."

"Housekeepers are just too slow and lazy. They don't care about guests. All they want to do is get through the day and go home. They don't care about the pressure we're under down here."

"Dear management! Do you know why customer satisfaction is falling? If we don't communicate between each other, don't you think that the guests are going to notice that?"

"When someone is missing a pillow or a towel it takes forever to get them to the room, which makes all of us look terrible. You can't hide this stuff from guests."

"Dan is telling us to cut labor. Jane and Robert tell us to schedule as many Front Desk agents as needed to provide quality service."

"Those maids make so much in tips and have no clue how difficult our job is; let's outsource housekeeping."

Here are some of the issues highlighted by Housekeeping employees:

- Bad information from the Front Desk about priorities for guest rooms.

- Last-minute surprises about large groups checking into the hotel at the same time (they used to have all-staff meetings before arrival of a big group.)

- Unwillingness of Front Desk and Concierge employees to pitch in outside their specific job responsibilities during busy times.

- Poor treatment of housekeeping staff by Front Desk crew. Where does the lack of respect issue come from? And how big of a problem is it? I think it's fairly typical for the Guest Services people downstairs to see us . . . as being less important than they are. It's not completely unique.

- Yeah, but why should we work hard, anyway? We don't get many tips. And even if we bust our butts and turn our rooms around quickly, no one really appreciates us.

- It's no wonder two of our best housekeepers left us last month. And no one ever helps us. You'd think one of the guys in the monkey suits standing downstairs might come upstairs every once in a while and vacuum or something.

- Those Front Desk clerks, they don't talk to housekeepers upstairs until there's an emergency. And by then, it's too late. And when the emergency is over, they don't even think to go upstairs and say thank you. It's like they're too good or something. And when they call us, they act like we're second-class citizens. They look down at us. We're the ones who have to keep this beautiful hotel in good shape.

- Rooms are not ready on time because no one downstairs tells anyone upstairs which rooms they need first.

Minutes after Dan received the results, he also got two voice mails, one from Judith and another one from Shakia.

Judith left the following message: "Dan, can you believe those maids? What do you want me to learn from them? I will stop by later. Bye."

Shakia said: "Hi Dan. I guess you received it too. Don't you think Judith and her team have a silo[1] mentality? You know that my people work very hard and they know what their priorities are. Can I come to see you?"

1. Describe the situation in the Rooms Division.

2. Identify some underlying reasons for the situation.

3. Highlight some consequences that the situation causes.

4. What can be done to tear down silos and reduce conflicts and increase collaboration?

Your action plan should be organized as follows:

    a. Strategic decisions (culture/"big picture")
    b. Organizational structure/work design
    c. Programs aimed at fostering cooperation/prevent workgroup arrogance
    d. Performance management
    e. Rooms division policies and procedures

Note

[1]Silo Mentality

Team members perceive their role in the organization purely in terms of the activities within their own, specific department (silo).

Reference

This case is inspired by situations described in:

Lencioni, P. (2006). *Silos, politics, and turf wars.* San Francisco: Jossey-Bass.

Notes and Responses to Case Questions:

Taking Corrective Actions

Image © Nicholas Sutcliffe, 2009. Used under license from Shutterstock.com

Choosing the Right Level of Discipline

Case Type:	**Application Case**
Main Subjects:	**Coaching, Discipline**
Who's Who:	• Shakia Andrews, *Executive Housekeeper*
	• Blake Cassara, *Houseman*
	• Betty Chu, *Human Resources Manager*
	• Yvonne Clark, *Director of Sales and Marketing*
	• Wesley Edwards, *Room Service Manager*
	• Kelsey Garber, *PBX Operator*
	• Henry Hermann, *Houseman*
	• Robert Kunz, *General Manager*
	• Cassidy Mei, *Sales Coordinator*
	• Katherine Norton, *Director of Human Resources*
	• Louise Rausch, *Director of Finance*
	• Kalinda Stenton, *PBX Manager*

"When dealing with an employee problem," explained Katherine during the last management outing, "progressive discipline requires you to follow these steps: coaching, verbal warning, written warning, suspension, and finally termination. The trick is to figure out when coaching is the right response and when more serious discipline is in order."

Managers from various departments were asked to write down a few recent disciplinary issues. During coffee break, Katherine and Betty quickly reviewed the situations and asked some managers to present their stories to the entire team as managerial dilemmas.

Here are the situations the Human Resource team selected.

a. "What's fairest way to discipline these two employees?" asked Shakia. "In Housekeeping, I caught two housemen, Henry and Blake, trying on guest shoes together in the shoeshine area. Henry hasn't needed to be disciplined before, but Blake was reprimanded recently for sitting on the bed in an occupied room. Should Blake's discipline be more severe than Henry's?"

b. "In Accounting," continued Mike, "the night auditor once used the wrong formula on the daily revenue report and sent Louise the document with unrealistic, inflated Average Daily Revenue figures."

c. "In PBX, we had a policy breach case," remembered Kalinda. "A new employee, Kelsey, was listening to her iPod while answering the calls. Customers were complaining that they heard loud music and were distracted while talking to the operator. Kelsey forgot to review the operations manual, even though it was included in her orientation package."

d. "A few years back the Room Service assistant manager shared with one of our servers all the details of a discrimination investigation concerning the Room Service order taker," added Wesley.

e. "I told Cassidy, our sales coordinator," said Yvonne, "that I needed a competitive analysis ready by Thursday. On Thursday, at 6:30 P.M., Cassidy placed the document in my mail box. At that time I had already left for the day, and I was en route to the regional sales conference, starting on Friday. This analysis was part of my morning presentation. Since Cassidy didn't leave the report to my attention before the end of the shift, and did not follow up with an e-mail to me, I definitely wanted to sit down with her. I was wondering if discipline was warranted," asked Yvonne.

"Typically, our progressive discipline system entitles employees to three written warnings in a twelve-month period before suspension. We try to stick to this guideline but, to be honest with you, occasionally I decide to 'give the guy one more chance' after a final warning. That's the reason I like the flexibility of progressive discipline," Mr. Kunz added to the discussion.

1. What are the advantages of progressive discipline?
2. Help the managers choose the right response.
3. How do you evaluate Mr. Kunz's practice?

Reference
Inspired by situations described in:
Mader-Clark, M., & Guerin, L. (2007). *The Progressive Discipline Handbook.* Berkeley, CA: Nolo.

Notes and Responses to Case Questions:

age © Zsolt Nyulaszi, 2009. Used under license from
utterstock.com

Emily's Letters

Case Type:	**Application Case**
Main Subjects:	**Anger, Coaching, Discipline, Feedback**
Who's Who:	• Eddy Bucks, *Restaurant Server*
	• Betty Chu, *Human Resources Manager*
	• Emily Perkins, *Lounge and Bar Manager*
	• Bonifacio da Silva, *Restaurant Server*

This holiday morning, Emily was working on two different disciplinary warning letters. Earlier, she had gone down to Human Resource, where she was surprised to find Betty decorating the corridor. Betty graciously showed her the employee files and gave her a copy of the employee handbook. "Please make sure that you send me a copy of the letters, so that I can place them in their files," Betty said to her, "and don't forget the fireworks and concert on the banks of the Bedford River tonight," added Betty as she was leaving the office.

Emily looked confident and satisfied as she glanced at the documents on her desk. Recently, she attended a training seminar where they were provided with a checklist on how to document disciplinary actions. Because the lounge seemed to be quiet, she decided to sit down briefly with the two employees, first with Eddy and then with Bonifacio.

1. What are the advantages of proper documentation?

2. What are the dangers of overdocumenting?

3. Based on the two memos, analyze Emily's documentation technique. What mistakes is she making?

4. Please correct the memos accordingly.

5. Assume that Bonifacio responds angrily to the discipline. How do you think Emily should deal with him?

EXHIBITS

LETTER 1

Memorandum

Date: July 4, 2008

From: Emily Perkins

To: Eddy Bucks

Subject: Punctuality

Eddy, this letter will document our conversation on June 20, 2008, which raised my concern about your recent punctuality record. Over the last eighteen months you have been repeatedly tardy.

Unfortunately, now you were late again. When I asked you if everything was alright and if there was any specific reason about as to why you were late, you answered "I was running late because I had trouble starting my car." Eddy, we both know that this is just a bunch of baloney. It is a common courtesy to your coworkers for you to show up for work on time. Please remember that employees who are always tardy put an extra burden on their coworkers.

After your previous tardiness, I spoke with you and warned you that it cannot happen again. I later took my two weeks vacation and your next tardy arrival was noticed but apparently not documented by the new assistant manager. When I returned to see that the problem had persisted, I was simply shocked.

Previous actions have been taken when you were found drinking soda in front of guests on January 2, 2008 and when your name tag was missing on February 2, 2008. Certainly these other policy violations and your recent tardiness have made me go to the next level of disciplinary action.

This letter is to serve as a formal write-up. A copy of this document will be forwarded to the general manager. Eddy, your punctuality should be improved. As you know, Mother Emily is always here to come up with a great schedule for everybody. We all make mistakes; the reason for this letter is not to scare you or threaten you. However, if this occurs again, you will be disciplined again.

Sincerely,

Emily Perkins

_____

EMPLOYEE'S SIGNATURE

I have read and fully understand this notice.

(Note: Your signature is not required if you disagree with the contents of this document.)

LETTER 2

Memorandum

Date: July 4, 2008
From: Emily Perkins
To: Bonifacio da Silva
Subject: Suspension

The subject of this letter is to inform you of your gross misconduct yesterday.

As discussed, you left the floor without informing your fellow servers or a manager that you needed to step away.

Upon your return you were questioned as to your whereabouts and you informed me that you were needed at the concierge desk. Later you engaged in an argument with a colleague and you started harassing him.

Bonifacio, you can't just leave the restaurant without talking to anyone. Furthermore, harassing others is completely against company policy and will not be tolerated. In response to your actions, many of our guests were dissatisfied. This was the second time something like this has come up. I personally addressed this issue with you earlier, and clearly notified you that if it were happen again, you would surely be suspended.

As a result of your actions you will be suspended without pay effective tomorrow, Saturday, July 5, 2008.

Once again, you are expected to comply with our customer service standards. In order to ensure this does not happen again, I highly recommend that you attend a customer service training seminar.

Your length of service with the Royal Hotel indicates you are valuable to the company. I trust that you will benefit from this experience and make the necessary adjustments. However, if it happens again, you will you will be suspended for three days.

Sincerely,

Emily Perkins

_____

EMPLOYEE'S SIGNATURE

(Your signature means only that you have been advised of the contents of this warning. It does not signify that you agree with its contents.)

Incident Summary 1—Eddy's File

DATE	INCIDENT	ACTION
January 14, 2007	Tardy	Coaching discussion (Documentation of conversation attached)
January 28, 2007	Tardy	Verbal warning (attached)
January 2, 2008	Drinking soda in front of guests	Coaching discussion (Documentation of conversation attached)
February 2, 2008	Name tag missing	Verbal warning (attached)
February 15, 2008	Tardy	Coaching discussion (Documentation of conversation attached)
February 20, 2008	Tardy	Verbal warning (attached)

Incident Summary 2—Bonifacio's File

DATE	INCIDENT	ACTION
August 18, 2007	Grooming issue	Coaching discussion (Documentation of conversation attached)
August 19, 2007	Grooming issue	Verbal warning (attached)
September 25, 2007	Grooming issue	Written warning (attached)
September 27, 2007	Grooming issue	One day suspension (attached)
May, 20 2008	Left floor without authorization	Written warning (attached)

Royal Hotel—Employee Handbook (Excerpts)

ATTENDANCE AND PUNCTUALITY

- Attendance is a key factor in your job performance. Punctuality and regular attendance are expected of all employees.
- If you are absent for any reason, you must notify your supervisor as far in advance as possible.
- If you are unable to report on time, contact your supervisor directly, three hours before your scheduled shift.
- If you are unable to contact your supervisor directly, please contact Human Resources or Security. Do not leave a message with other employees.
- Employees who have excessive absenteeism or tardiness from work, even with acceptable excuses, are subject to discipline.
- Excessive absences or tardiness will be grounds for discipline up to and including termination.
- Any employee who does not report to work or call in to the employee's supervisor or Human Resources for three consecutive working days, is considered to have voluntarily resigned without notice.

STANDARDS OF CONDUCT

The Royal Hotel has adopted a progressive discipline policy to identify and address employee and employment-related problems. Preceding termination the following progressive discipline actions will be performed given the nature of the offence (serious offences such as physical or sexual assault and/or theft will have zero tolerance)—verbal warnings, written warnings, suspensions, and termination. While the Royal Hotel will generally take disciplinary action in a progressive manner, it reserves the right, in its sole discretion, to decide whether and what disciplinary action will be taken in a given situation. No disciplinary action may be used against an employee that is more than twelve months old.

Documentation Rules—Checklist

1. **Introduction**
2. **Nature of Problem**

2/a. Supporting Details (if appropriate)

3. **Rules/Policies That Have Been Violated**

3/a. Negative Impact on the Organization (if appropriate)

4. **History of Past Coaching or Corrective Actions**
5. **Disciplinary Action**
6. **Goals and Expectations**

6/a. Training or Special Direction (if appropriate)

6/b. Follow-Up/Feedback (if appropriate)

7. **Positive Statement**
8. **Consequences**
9. **Employee Section**

References

Falcone, P. (2000). A blueprint for progressive discipline and terminations. *HR Magazine, 77*(8), 3–5.

Roper, B. (n.d.). *A Step-by-Step Guide to Performance Documents.* Retrieved December 23, 2007, from Mott Community College Web site: http://www.mcc.edu/hr_protected/pdf/articles_performance_documents.pdf

Notes and Responses to Case Questions:

Case 47

Toby's Silence

Case Type:	**Head Case**
Main Subjects:	**Coaching, Defensiveness, Discipline, Feedback, Rapport**
Who's Who:	• Toby Kenney, *Purchasing Receiving Clerk*
	• Paul Bello, *Purchasing Manager*
	• Pascal Gateau, *Executive Chef*

Chef Gateau angrily called Paul in Purchasing early in the afternoon. He had ordered 40 pounds of product from "Western Quality Meats." However, when the butcher opened the box, he only found 30 pounds of the product.

The chef needed special imported steaks for a corporate event tonight. "I already took care of this; the chef of the Promenade Hotel will help me out this time," said the chef. "You know, Paul, it's not the first time this has happened. Please, take some action," the chef finished.

Receiving clerks were required to weigh all meat, fish, and poultry delivered to the Royal Hotel. Paul asked Toby, the receiving clerk, to come to his office.

"What is it about?" asked Toby.

"Please sit down Toby," answered Paul. "The chef called. Ten pounds of steak is apparently missing from the special order. I am sure you know that it is important that the Royal Hotel pays only for products that have been delivered," Paul continued.

Toby folded his arms around his chest firmly and was biting his lips.

"Do you realize that the chef did not have enough steak to prepare a special menu for tonight?" Paul asked him. Toby responded with stony silence.

"I expect a response. Actually, if you don't answer this minute, I will have to presume that you did not weigh the meat," added Paul.

Toby did not say anything—instead, he gazed down at his lap, appearing not to hear the discussion.

1. What can be the reasons behind an employee's silence during a disciplinary meeting?

2. How should managers generally deal with silent employees?

3. How would you evaluate Paul's last statement?

4. It seems that Toby does not care about the discussion. What are Paul's options?

Reference

Inspired by a situation described in:

Mader-Clark, M., & Guerin, L. (2007). *The Progressive Discipline Handbook* (pp. 186–191). Berkeley, CA: Nolo.

Notes and Responses to Case Questions:

When Employees Are Challenging Your Leadership

Image © Robyn Mackenzie, 2009. Used under license from
Shutterstock.com

I Have Plans for Tonight

Case Type:	**Incident Case**
Main Subjects:	**Authority, Buy-In, Controlling Costs, Discipline, Flexibility, Insubordination, Productivity**
Who's Who:	• Jimmy Britton, *Valet Parker*
	• Carlos Diaz, *Guest Services Manager*
	• Eduardo Sullivan, *Valet Parker*

Carlos was very concerned. Jimmy, one of the P.M. valet parkers, called in sick at 10 A.M. The Royal Hotel was expected to be fully booked this evening, and Carlos knew that Jimmy needed to be replaced. He contacted all part-time and on-call employees; no one was available.

Carlos paged Eduardo, who had just finished parking a car and asked him on the phone if he could stay longer. "I am sorry that Jimmy called in sick, but I have plans for tonight," answered Eduardo.

"It's your turn Eduardo; others did more overtime this month. The hotel policy says I have to give you three hours notice for overtime. I'm giving you four. If you don't stay, I will write you up." With this, Carlos ended the conversation.

1. Under what circumstances can a supervisor authorize overtime?

2. Can employers require employees to work overtime?

3. How should overtime be distributed?

4. What should Carlos have done differently?

5. How can you minimize the likelihood of a similar situation from reoccurring?

Notes and Responses to Case Questions:

Image © fotosav, 2009. Used under license from Shutterstock.com

The Tipping Issue

Case Type:	**Head Case**
Main Subjects:	**Authority, Discipline**
Who's Who:	• Emily Perkins, *Lounge and Bar Manager*
	• Laura Daley, *Restaurant Server*

"Sorry Emily," Laura said, her voice raised, "these are the same people who did not leave a tip after I served them last week. I am not serving them!"

Emily seated the party quickly in another server's section, so that the guests did not notice the incident. The Lounge got very busy suddenly, and she could not deal with the issue until the end of her shift. Emily knew that servers are paid a low hourly rate and they rely on tips. As a former server she was compassionate with the wait staff; however, she was unsure how to address this with Laura.

1. How would you, as Emily, deal with this situation?

2. What can Emily do to minimize the likelihood of a similar situation from reoccurring?

Notes and Responses to Case Questions:

That's Not My Job!

Case Type:	**Incident Case**
Main Subjects:	**Authority, Discipline, Insubordination, Job Design/Job Description**
Who's Who:	• George Kramer, *Restaurant Guest*
	• Carmen Meadors, *Restaurant Server*
	• Jennifer Ortiz, *Restaurant Manager*

The last breakfast guest, Mr. Kramer, was leisurely reading a newspaper in the restaurant and the large clock showed noon when he departed. Once he had left, Jennifer asked Carmen, one of the servers, to quickly remove the silver-plated jam stands from the tables.

Carmen's response was "No," stating that it was not her job; it was a server assistant's responsibility. At this time Jennifer asked her again to collect a tray and remove the jam stands from the tables and Carmen replied again, "No. I'm already stretching the limits of my job description without any compensation." Jennifer asked her a third time to clear the jams stands, and again the server reiterated that she would not complete this task. Because the first lunch guests were ready to be seated, Jennifer had to run quickly to the front to give the host person a hand. Carmen walked back to the kitchen to serve fresh bread to the arriving guests. The lunch was busy; the jam stands were sitting on the tables for at least another hour until they were finally removed.

In the meantime, Jennifer decided to have a "heart-to-heart" with Carmen once this busy lunch was over.

1. What constitutes insubordination?
2. Identify potential reasons for employees engaging in insubordinate conduct.
3. When can an employee refuse to obey an order?
4. Is disciplinary action warranted? What should Jennifer have done differently?
5. Why should we suspend employees as a final step of our progressive discipline system?

Notes and Responses to Case Questions:

Case 51

They Can Wait!

Case Type:	**Incident Case**
Main Subjects:	**Authority, Discipline, Insubordination**
Who's Who:	• Steven Kinzer, *Restaurant Server*
	• Jennifer Ortiz, *Restaurant Manager*

A little bit before noon Jennifer seated a new guest. She had to seek Steven, the server, out in the back service pantry to inform him that he had a table. Jennifer noticed that during service the same guest had to flag Steven twice to get more coffee.

Later, another table expressed its displeasure because it had not been approached by a server. Jennifer went to the back and found Steven reading a newspaper. Jennifer told him to go to the table right away. While Steven closed the newspaper slowly, he responded by saying "Yeah, yeah. I'm going. I'm going. Just relax. Take a Valium."

1. Would you consider Steven's actions as insubordination?

2. If you were Jennifer, what would you do?

Notes and Responses to Case Questions:

Case 52

Barbara Is Going Over My Head

Case Type:	Issue Case
Main Subjects:	Authority, Chain of Command, Credibility, Open-Door Policy, Organizational Structure, Trust
Who's Who:	• Lori Canelle, *Spa Manager*
	• Dan Mazur, *Director of Rooms*
	• Barbara Turner, *Spa Employee*

After the Raynsford family left the Spa, Barbara approached Lori and expressed her concern about the pool temperature. According to her the Raynsford kids found the pool too cold. Barbara suggested that Lori should slightly increase the pool temperature.

"Listen Barbara," said Lori, "I appreciate your ideas, but according to our standards the pool temperature should be in the range of 78–80 degrees Fahrenheit."

"Don't worry Lori," answered Barbara, "I will just go and see Dan; he knows his stuff and will fix this problem." At this point Barbara left the Spa to see the director of Rooms. The Royal Hotel had an open-door policy designed to encourage employees to communicate their concerns or suggestions to their direct supervisors and also to provide them with the option of carrying their problems to senior management without fear of retaliation.

When Lori came back after her two days off, she noticed that Engineering slightly adjusted the temperature of the pool.

1. What are some of the potential benefits open-door policies offer?

2. What can be some of the drawbacks and implications of violating the chain of command?

    a. From the employee's perspective

    b. From the first-line supervisor's perspective

    c. From an organizational perspective

3. Determine probable reasons for Dan's actions.

4. How do you think Dan should have dealt with the situation?

Notes and Responses to Case Questions:

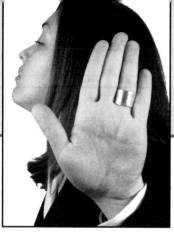
Image © Andresr, 2009. Used under license from Shutterstock.com

I Am Just Not Comfortable Talking to You!

Case Type:	**Head Case**
Main Subjects:	**Authority, Discipline, Insubordination, Open-Door Policy**
Who's Who:	• Rose Romero, *PBX Operator*
	• Kalinda Stenton, *PBX Manager*

As Kalinda came back from her break, she witnessed a serious conduct infraction involving Rose, one of the PBX operators. She immediately asked someone to cover the phone and asked Rose to come with her and discuss the situation in her office.

At this point Rose looked at her and said, "You know Kalinda, I am sorry, but I am just not comfortable talking to you."

Kalinda paused for a second and told Rose, "I'm sorry to hear about your discomfort, who are you comfortable talking to?" Rose's answer was, "I will take care of this. I know my rights Kalinda."

Rather than insisting that employees stay within chains of command when they have unresolved problems, the Royal Hotel promoted an open-door policy, in which employees were encouraged to talk to any manager with whom they felt comfortable speaking.

1. Would you consider Rose's actions appropriate? Why? Why not?
2. What could Kalinda have done differently?

Notes and Responses to Case Questions:

Case 54

I Don't Have
Time to Talk to You

Case Type:	**Head Case**
Main Subjects:	**Assertiveness, Authority, Credibility, Defensiveness, Discipline, Insubordination, Respect**
Who's Who:	• Judith Grace, *Front Office Manager*
	• Randy Maguire, *Front Desk Agent*
	• Kristianne Tyler, *Regular Hotel Guest*

A s Judith entered the Front Office area she noticed that Randy, one of the agents, greeted Ms. Tyler, a regular guest, in an unprofessional and unfriendly manner. She was visibly in a hurry and asked politely if she could go up to her room to make a quick phone call and come back to complete the check-in process in a few minutes. Randy raised his voice and responded by saying, "I am working as fast as I can."

Judith waited until Ms. Tyler had left the Front Desk before she approached Randy. Judith pulled him to the side and asked him to come to see her in the back office. At this point, Randy raised his voice and told her, "I don't have time to talk to you.... I am serving my guests! I was hired to make sure our customers are happy!" and he walked back to the desk to check in the next guest in line.

When the next customer left, Judith attempted to confront Randy again, without any success. She stood in the corner for a few more minutes, feeling brushed off.

1. Would you consider Randy's answer to Judith appropriate? Why? Why not?

2. Determine probable reasons for Randy's behavior with Judith.

3. What could Judith have done differently when she witnessed the situation?

4. Is disciplinary action warranted?

Notes and Responses to Case Questions:

I Know My Stuff!

Case Type:	**Incident Case**
Main Subjects:	**Authority, Change, Credibility, Defensiveness, Discipline, Respect, Trust**
Who's Who:	• Wesley, Edwards, *Room Service Manager*
	• Adam Warren, *Room Service Server*

Wesley graduated from a hospitality program three years ago. He joined the Royal Hotel as a management trainee in Food and Beverage. Six months later he became an assistant manager in the Lounge. Recently he was promoted to Room Service manager. He was very enthusiastic about this great opportunity and started in his position with great deal of energy.

This morning, he decided to shadow the servers in order to familiarize himself with the service process. Wesley entered the elevator, greeted Adam, the front server, and offered his help. Adam answered by saying, "You know, Wesley, I know my stuff. I was doing this job before you were born. I don't need any guidance here."

"I hate to tell you this, but I will spend the day with you," responded Wesley and he pushed the "door-close" button.

1. Determine probable reasons for Adam's behavior.
2. Evaluate the response of Wesley in the elevator.
3. If you were in Wesley's position, what would your next step be?
4. What could Wesley have done to prevent this situation from happening?

Notes and Responses to Case Questions:

Image © Robert Wróblewski, 2009. Used under license from Shutterstock.com

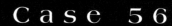

He Couldn't Find His Office Without a Map!

Case Type:	**Incident Case**
Main Subjects:	**Authority, Credibility, Gossip, Managing Up, Organizational Politics**
Who's Who:	• Paul Bello, *Purchasing Manager*
	• Romero Barnes, *Assistant Purchasing Manager*
	• Yuan Yao, *Assistant Director of Finance*

A few managers from various finance departments began to gather in the cafeteria. Romero, the assistant purchasing manager, was speaking about his serious difficulties with one of the wine suppliers. Someone asked him if Paul had already been involved.

"Paul? You don't honestly think anyone's going to take him seriously? He couldn't find his office without a map!" answered Romero in a sarcastic, belittling tone.

None of them noticed that Paul was in the cafeteria and overheard the entire discussion. As Paul proceeded to the coffee machine, he quickly turned back and saw that Yuan was still smiling.

1. Evaluate Romero's behavior.

2. What advice would you give to Paul?

3. What could have been done differently to prevent this situation from happening?

4. The difference between unacceptable public criticism and acceptable disagreement lies in the setting and the manner of presentation. Explain.

Notes and Responses to Case Questions:

Relationship with Your Boss

Image © Feverpitch, 2009. Used under license from Shutterstock.com

My Way or the Highway

Case Type:	**Head Case**
Main Subjects:	**Big Picture, Delegation, Hands-On, Managing Up, Micromanagement, Perfectionism, Trust**
Who's Who:	• Yvonne Clark, *Director of Sales and Marketing*
	• Fiona O'Brien, *Public Relations Manager*
	• Luke O'Brien, *Fiona's Husband*

Fiona was desperate. She recently joined the Royal Hotel as the Public Relations manager. Although she found the job rewarding, after six months in her job, she felt trapped and somewhat betrayed. She remembered her first discussion with her future boss, Yvonne, the director of Sales and Marketing. "I will do what is necessary to ensure your success. I was the Public Relations manager upon opening this hotel and I built everything from scratch. I would like to make your job easier by sharing my experience and knowledge," she explained to Fiona. "But no worries—I'm not a micro." Yvonne added jokingly.

Last night, at home, Luke, Fiona's husband, was gently questioning her about why she was so depressed lately. Finally, Fiona shared with him some of her concerns:

Yvonne has very high standards and wants detailed progress reports on her projects twice a day. At the same time, she doesn't delegate any work of real significance to Fiona.

Even low-level decisions (like selecting photos for media requests) must be approved by Yvonne.

The other day, Yvonne was home with the flu and she still called Fiona twice during the day.

Yvonne watches Fiona's every move; last week Fiona was on the phone with a local reporter when Yvonne showed up, sat down, and listened to what Fiona was saying.

"I just don't feel in control of anything. Does that make sense?" Fiona asked.

1. Identify potential causes for Yvonne's behavior.
2. Highlight some consequences that such situations cause. What is the underlying leadership issue?
3. What do you think Fiona should do about this matter?
4. What advice would you give to Yvonne?

Notes and Responses to Case Questions:

Image © Serghei Starus, 2009. Used under license from Shutterstock.com

The Buffet Setup

Case Type: Issue Case

Main Subjects: Authority, Chain of Command, Credibility, Managing Up, Open-Door Policy, Organizational Politics

Who's Who:
- Jeff Gillespie, *Assistant Banquet Manager*
- Monica Luigi, *Guest, On-Site Contact*
- Rhiannon Palmer, *Convention Services Manager*
- Jane Peterson, *Hotel Manager*
- Thomas Waxer, *Banquet Manager*

Ms. Luigi, the on-site contact, was very disappointed and upset with the dinner setup for her pharmaceutical group. She originally arranged with Rhiannon for two, double-sided buffets for the dinner, because the group was on a tight time schedule. Earlier today, due to the slight decrease in attendee numbers, Thomas, the Banquet manager, decided to set up one double-sided buffet for the group, without informing Ms. Luigi in advance. Thomas was the opening manager, and left for the day around 3 P.M. Jeff, the assistant manager, professionally dealt with Ms. Luigi. He profusely apologized and offered free ice cream for the entire group.

After the group left, Jeff picked up the phone; after a moment's hesitation he dialed the Hotel manager's extension and left the following voice mail:

"Hi Jane, this is Jeff from Banquets. This is regarding the in-house pharmaceutical group. Unfortunately, Ms. Luigi was very angry tonight because of the wrong dinner setup. It seems that Thomas did not read the Banquet Event Order properly. By the way he left early today, so I could not discuss this with him. I know how much revenue this group brings, so I felt it is my responsibility to make sure that you know exactly what's going on. See you tomorrow. Bye."

Rather than insisting that employees stay within chains of command when they have unresolved problems, the Royal Hotel promoted an open-door policy, in which employees were encouraged to talk to any manager with whom they felt comfortable talking.

1. Why do employees often go above their own boss? Why do others never bypass?
2. What are the pros and cons of allowing employees to talk to any manager at any level about any issue?
3. How do you explain Jeff's behavior?
4. What do you think Jane should do about this matter?

Notes and Responses to Case Questions:

Image © Scott David Patterson, 2009. Used under license from Shutterstock.com

Lipstick on the Glass

Case Type:	**Issue Case**
Main Subjects:	**Authority, Chain of Command, Influence, Managing Up**
Who's Who:	• Margot Cooper, *Hotel Guest*
	• John Ferreira, *Chief Steward*
	• Bruce Koss, *Assistant Chief Steward*
	• Jane Peterson, *Hotel Manager*

Jane had a few minutes before the start of the morning meeting, so she quickly reviewed the daily guest incident report. "At checkout Ms. Cooper mentioned that the martini glass with which she was served at the bar last night had lipstick and ugly white spots on it." This glitch made Jane really angry.

"Once again, Stewarding, I really need to talk to those guys in person," Jane said as she was walking down the kitchen corridor.

After a very busy back-to-back shift, Bruce, the new assistant manager, was sitting in the Stewarding Office, about to do the labor forecast, when Jane entered.

"Standard No. 1," Jane pointed to the stewarding key expectations posted on the wall, "Stewarding should ensure customers never see a dirty dish."

"So, what are we doing about this martini glass issue?" Jane smiled.

Bruce was unsure and said he would look into the problem.

"Minerals in hard water can cause white film deposits and ugly spots to build up on glasses in the dishwasher," Jane was lecturing Bruce. "To match the hardness of the water, please increase the amount of detergent by 25%." Jane provided Bruce with specific instructions and went to the morning meeting. Several hours later, John, the chief steward who worked in the P.M. shift, noticed that someone had adjusted the amount of detergent used.

"Jane Peterson told me to do it." Bruce said to him.

"What? We can't just change the amount of detergent!" John was fuming. "Bruce, I left you a message yesterday morning in the log book explaining that there is a loss of water pressure because of pump obstruction and martini glasses needed to be handwashed until further instruction." John added.

1. How can leaders influence the development and effectiveness of individuals that are not reporting directly to them?
2. Managers often engage in direct one-to-one relationships with supervisors at lower levels of organizations beyond their direct reports. Why?
3. Identify problems Jane's action is causing.
4. What would you recommend John do?

Notes and Responses to Case Questions:

Alison, The Credit Manager

Case Type:	Head Case
Main Subjects:	Influence, Motivation, Organizational Politics, Promotion
Who's Who:	• Piet Brown, *Hotel Guest*
	• Yvonne Clark, *Director of Sales and Marketing*
	• Alison Finley, *Credit Manager*
	• Charlie Jones, *Director of Engineering*
	• Matthew Knorr, *Director of Food and Beverage*
	• Robert Kunz, *General Manager*
	• Sylvain Lucas, *Local Party Planner*
	• Dan Mazur, *Director of Rooms*
	• Katherine Norton, *Director of Human Resources*
	• Jane Peterson, *Hotel Manager*
	• Louise Rausch, *Director of Finance*
	• Yuan Yao, *Assistant Director of Finance*

L ouise Rausch was preparing herself for the next succession planning meeting. "They will definitely spend some time on the Credit Manager," she thought. Alison recently expressed her interest in becoming the assistant director of Finance, if the position becomes available.

Executive committee members all had something to say about Alison. Here are some quotes from the meeting minutes:

Louise: Whenever Yuan is asking Alison to work on a project, she e-mails him back the completed assignments in a timely manner. However, I noticed that she always copies me on the correspondence.

Katherine: I asked her opinion about the development plan we put together for the Finance interns. Alison said that, as a team player, she was not here to criticize management's ideas; she prefers going with flow and making things happen.

Dan: Last week, after the Budget meeting, she told me that my presentation on the Rooms Division had inspired her so much that she is now considering a career change. I am wondering if she really wants to stay in Finance.

Yvonne: At the same meeting, Alison proudly announced that she managed the returned check from the Brown party. Well, I called Piet Brown personally and asked him to mail us a new check.

Matthew: I asked her to review the direct billing request of Sylvain Lucas, a local party planner. It took her six weeks to determine their eligibility and credit limits. She claimed that it's a complex issue, and she is working hard to get an answer. Is Alison procrastinating?

Charlie: I see her only twice a month. She is systematically late for the safety meeting. Her verbiage is always the same: Charlie, please forgive me, I know your time is valuable.

Jane: May I make a quick note on Matthew's observation? I am not sure about that. I have a very different experience in terms of her follow-through skills. Last November, I asked her to circulate the invitation to the credit management training workshop. She actually did it very efficiently. I was only curious why she changed the layout of the original document and placed the application form at the very end of the e-mail. I wondered why she included 20 pages of additional background information on credit management before the application form as well, making it almost impossible to find.

Robert: I don't know guys. I perceive Alison as a warm and supporting individual. She loves my ideas on how to deal with payment problems. Last month she even circulated a musical card—playing my favorite song—for all managers to sign for my birthday.

1. Evaluate Alison as a manager.
2. What are the pros and cons of praising those with more power?
3. What are the pros and cons of self-promotion tactics in the workplace?
4. Why do workplace politics have a bad connotation? What can management do to change this negative perception?
5. Assume that you are hired by the Royal Hotel as a management trainee. You will have to attend a four-day management orientation program. What actions would you take to promote yourself and emerge as a potential leader?

Notes and Responses to Case Questions:

The New Table Pickup System

Case Type:	**Head Case**
Main Subjects:	**Authority, Chain of command, Coaching, Credibility, Feedback, Managing Up, Open-Door Policy, Organizational Politics**
Who's Who:	• Wesley Edwards, *Room Service Manager*
	• Matthew Knorr, *Director of Food and Beverage*
	• Danielle Rosenthal, *Room Service Assistant Manager*

After a busy breakfast service, Danielle, the assistant manager, approached Wesley. "Listen, Wes, as you know, I have worked in various hotels and know something about room service. To be honest, every hotel has a hard time coming up with an efficient table retrieval technique. I think the new table pickup system you implemented here is great. We are receiving fewer complaints and dirty trays have basically disappeared from the corridors."

"I truly appreciate your feedback Danielle, we all need to work together and consistently stick to this new procedure," answered Wesley. "By the way, as you suggested, we will be placing a computer in front of the service elevator in order to track the status of retrievals," he added.

Later, on the same day, the following conversation occurred between Danielle and Matthew:

DANIELLE: Do you have a moment for a poor middle manager?

MATTHEW: (laughing) Sure, come on in.

DANIELLE: What I really like here at the Royal is that we can talk to any manager we feel comfortable talking to.

MATTHEW: (smiling) Of course, we are proud of our open-door policy. What can I do for you?

DANIELLE: I think you should know what's happening in Room Service.

MATTHEW: (still smiling) Should I?

DANIELLE: It's about Wesley. He changed the table retrieval system, and I am worried that it will negatively affect the level of service.

MATTHEW: (unsure) Yeah, I don't think our pickup system was the most efficient one …

DANIELLE: This new system is wrong and highly distracting for servers, but you know, Matthew, this is not the main issue. Wesley doesn't involve us in anything; he just doesn't appreciate ideas, which is, in my mind, the opposite of how a Royal manager should behave. He is lacking people skills, and the morale is down in room service.

MATTHEW: (hesitating) Have you discussed your concern with Wesley?

DANIELLE: I was not comfortable doing it … and I thought it's work related so I came to see you …

MATTHEW: (somewhat annoyed) Your feedback is important; thank you for sharing it. I really thought that this new procedure was working well. It seems that we have to go back to the old system. Regarding Wesley; I guess you want me to serve as a referee between you and him.

DANIELLE: (uncertain) I guess, yes.

Matthew always wanted to deal with issues in the right way. At the same time, as Danielle was walking out from his office, he felt slightly confused and had a couple of questions on his mind.

1. Should managers pay attention to what others say about them when they are not present?

2. What is the major issue facing Matthew?

3. What motivation might Danielle have behind her action?

4. What mistakes is Matthew making, if any? How would you have handled the situation if you had been in Matthew's situation?

5. How can managers diminish the chances of being the object of manipulations?

6. How can exit interviews help Human Resource to pick up on signs of negative office politics?

Notes and Responses to Case Questions:

Case 62

The Missing Cancellation Clause

Case Type: Head Case

Main Subjects: Accepting Criticism, Assertiveness, Defensiveness, Feedback, Managing Up

Who's Who:
- Yvonne Clark, *Director of Sales and Marketing*
- Rhiannon Palmer, *Convention Services Manager*

This morning, Yvonne came back from the morning meeting with a piece of returned mail in her hand. The following conversation occurred between her and Rhiannon:

YVONNE: Rhiannon, this isn't the first group contract your people have sent out without the cancellation clause. If you don't start getting it right fast, there'll be trouble.

RHIANNON: Me? That's a joke. If only Sales wouldn't make so many errors. They should have gotten it right in the first place.

YVONNE: Your errors aren't just Sales-related. You leave Sales to me and worry about your own area.

RHIANNON: I'd worry a lot less about Convention Services if HR could hire more competent staff members.

YVONNE: You get the same people as everyone else. Have you ever thought of training them? No, too busy moaning. By the way, I created a new coordinator position for you and you're still complaining!

RHIANNON: I know … it's just that … well, there's not really enough time to train the new coordinator.

YVONNE: Well, that's for you to manage.

RHIANNON: I know. I'm sorry … . We try our best, but … well … there's just so much pressure at the moment.

YVONNE: We're all under pressure, Rhiannon. That's no excuse. What I want to know is what you are going to do about it, because if you don't get it sorted out, I will.

1. Highlight some of the benefits of being criticized.

2. What key mistakes is Rhiannon making?

3. An assertive person expresses his or her thoughts, feelings, and needs directly, while taking into account the rights and feelings of others. Describe assertive techniques for how Rhiannon should have answered initially and how she should have addressed the following issues:

   - There are errors in the contract; some of them are originated by Sales.
   - There is new coordinator in Convention Services.
   - Finding solutions.

Reference

This case is inspired by a situation described in:

Gillen, T. (1992). *Assertiveness for Managers* (pp. 107–117). Brookfield, VT: Gower.

Notes and Responses to Case Questions:

PART NINE

Managing a Diverse Workforce

Case 63

Why Diversity Matters

Case Type:	**Issue Case**
Main Subjects:	**Discrimination, Diversity**
Who's Who:	• Betty Chu, *Human Resources Manager*
	• John Ferreira, *Chief Steward*

B etty has recently joined the Royal Hotel as the new Human Resources manager. As part of her yearly action plan she has decided to set up a diversity committee. She invited some department heads and members of protected classes to join the first meeting next week. This morning Betty received the following e-mail from John, the chief steward.

E-Mail

Hello Betty,

Thanks for inviting me to join the diversity committee of the hotel.

Let me share some of my thoughts with you regarding this new committee.

Personally, I feel that the steps that need to be taken by minority workers are their own responsibility to take on. In this country it is illegal to discriminate based on race. Minority workers have the same opportunities as any other American workers, and the resources to learn English are readily available to everyone. It is up to the minority workers to take the initial step in recognizing that the English language is a necessary skill to be learned.

I have no worries that the minority workers (whom I respect as equally capable people) who want to become managers will indeed be successful here at the Royal Hotel.

I will stop by this afternoon to discuss this further.

Regards,
John

1. Some people believe that we should treat all employees equally regardless of their personal characteristics. Do you agree? Explain.

2. Some organizations require that members of protected classes sit on their diversity committee. What are the dangers of this practice?

3. What suggestions would you offer to Betty to set up the committee?

4. It has become common for companies to develop recruitment and selection programs that focus on achievement of a specific percentage for minority and employment. What are the risks in implementing such programs?

Notes and Responses to Case Questions:

The Levels of Exclusion

Case Type:	**Application Case**
Main Subjects:	**Bias, Discrimination, Diversity, Prejudice, Stereotypes**
Who's Who:	• Betty Chu, *Human Resources Manager*

The Royal's diversity committee was committed to systematically spotting hidden biases across the hotel. "We may avoid or exclude someone because of a belief that people from that group are inferior in some way. The problem is that if you bring together a group of Royal managers and say, 'OK, we're going to do antidiscrimination training—who has a prejudice?' my sense is people will raise their hand because people just aren't going to define themselves as a racist," said Betty.

"When they are accused of discrimination, people take great offense," added another manager.

"By the way guys, do we know what the difference is among stereotype, prejudice, and discrimination?" wondered one of the members in the committee.

To move forward, the committee decided that the members will listen and take note of suspicious comments and incidents about Latinos, for a month. According to the meeting minutes, "Based on the findings and to help employees face their biases, a future committee meeting will work out an action plan."

Here is the list of the statements and situations committee members collected during the month:

Employee Cafeteria

1. Are you looking for burritos, Dominga?

Food and Beverage

2. Hispanics like spicy foods.

3. I don't like Latinos like Francisco; they are taking our front-of-house jobs.

4. Jose is the chef? I'll have to talk loud and slow to make sure he is able understand me.

5. We shouldn't let Santos be in charge of the register. He might steal.

6. I don't think Enrique, the busboy, should be the new server; customers will think we can't afford American staff.

Rooms Division

7. Guest Services employees referred to Carlos as "that Mexican guy," when he is from Guatemala.

8. I avoid immigrants like Soledad from Housekeeping. They are illegal.

9. Luiz has been in the Laundry longer than other employees who are white, but gets paid less.

10. Esteban was not invited to the employees' Fourth of July party after work because they did not consider him to be American.

Engineering

11. Where is Cruz, the plumber? They have a "mañana" attitude.

12. Manuel must have only gotten the electrician job because they need to fulfill a quota.

13. Consuelo was not picked for a special renovation task because she couldn't speak English well.

SPA

14. Latino men are macho.

15. I wouldn't invite Jorge to play golf; they have low income.

Sales

16. I'll write this e-mail myself. His grammar is probably bad.

Royal Hotel Job Fair

17. They don't mind working for lower paying jobs.

18. They can't speak English well.

19. Ramana can be placed in a housekeeping position; this is where most Latinas are.

20. Let's place Ines in a less visible position.

1. What is the difference between stereotyping, prejudice, and discrimination?

2. How can hidden biases hurt our business?

3. Review the statements and situations and identify each as an example of stereotyping, prejudice, or discrimination.

4. How would you advise an employee who feels that his or her minority status is a stumbling block at work?

Reference

Babcock, P. (2006). Detecting hidden bias. *HR Magazine, 51*(2), 50–55.

Carr-Ruffino, N. (2005). *Making Diversity Work*. Upper Saddle River, NJ: Pearson Prentice Hall.

Notes and Responses to Case Questions:

Please Hire Him.
He Is Like Me!

Case Type:	**Head Case**
Main Subjects:	**Discrimination, Diversity, Recruiting/Selection**
Who's Who:	• Fred Poitier, *Banquet Server*
	• Thomas Waxer, *Banquet Manager*

Thomas, the Banquet manager, was looking at the list of open positions on the wall and sighed heavily. Business is picking up; they will most definitely need additional servers he thought to himself. Thomas was thinking about going down to Human Resource to see if there were any new applicants when the phone rang. It was Fred Poitier, one of the most experienced banquet servers.

"Hi Thomas. Is this referral bonus thing still going on? I would like to recommend my old buddy from back home. He just moved to the States and he is looking for a job. He is very nice and he could do the job," Fred told him.

"That's great Fred!" Thomas replied enthusiastically. "Why don't you just ask your friend to give me a call tomorrow?"

Most of the banquet servers at the Royal Hotel are of Haitian origin. They are all hardworking. Hiring another employee with the same background seemed to be a logical decision.

1. Should the manager just go ahead and interview the candidate? Why? Why not?

2. What are some of the pros and cons of using employee referrals?

3. How can employers avoid racial discrimination when recruiting and hiring?

4. How can Human Resource departments further minimize the likelihood of the "like-me bias" during the interview process?

Notes and Responses to Case Questions:

English Only

Case Type:	**Head Case**
Main Subjects:	**Discrimination, Diversity**
Who's Who:	• Katherine Norton, *Director of Human Resources*
	• Emily Perkins, *Lounge and Bar Manager*

Voice Mail

"Hi Katherine, this is Emily. We have an issue here at the Lounge. As you know, most of our employees are Hispanic and they tend to talk to each other in Spanish, although they are fluent in English. It really bothers me, and I believe guests find this offensive too.

Is it ok with you guys in Human Resource, if I establish an English only policy? I would love to start it on Monday. Thanks Katherine."

1. Can the Royal Hotel enforce a policy that requires all employees to speak English at all times?

2. What advice would you give to Katherine?

3. How can the Royal Hotel help employees who speak different languages work in harmony?

Notes and Responses to Case Questions:

Image © Junial Enterprises, 2009. Used under license from
Shutterstock.com

Can I Have Another Boss Please?

Case Type:	**Head Case**
Main Subjects:	**Coaching, Discrimination, Diversity**
Who's Who:	• Shakia Andrews, *Executive Housekeeper*
	• Patu Manga, *Houseman*
	• Katherine Norton, *Director of Human Resources*
	• Thomas Waxer, *Banquet Manager*

Shakia, the executive housekeeper, was rather happy today. Finally, she was able to fill all the open positions. Last week she hired Patu, a male employee, for the houseman position. Patu originally was also interested in an open banquet position, but he agreed with Thomas the Banquet manager that Housekeeping was the priority.

Patu has recently emigrated from an African country and seemed to be very happy in his new job. This afternoon Shakia received an e-mail from the Human Resource director notifying her that Patu is complaining that he is not comfortable being a subordinate to a female boss.

As Shakia was walking down to Human Resource, she was wondering how to handle the situation.

1. What actions could Shakia take before her meeting with Patu?

2. How would you address the situation with Patu?

3. What, if any, reasonable accommodation could be made that would enable Patu to successfully perform his job?

Notes and Responses to Case Questions:

Case 68

Can I Have Another Server Please?

Case Type:	**Head Case**
Main Subject:	**Discrimination, Diversity**
Who's Who:	• Mary Kim, *Room Service Order Taker*
	• Johnny Moerschell, *Assistant Room Service Manager*
	• Louis Nichols, *Room Service Server*
	• Peter Fischer, *Room Service Server*
	• Marc Watkins, *Hotel VIP Guest*

Mary, the Room Service order taker, took her dinner break, and Johnny, the assistant manager, covered for her. Just before the end of Mary's break Mr. Watkins's called from the Royal Suite to place his dinner order.

After Johnny repeated his order, Mr. Watkins added, "One more thing! May I request a white server?"

"I beg your pardon?" exclaimed Johnny.

"You know, I have nothing against African American people. I myself am a black man," replied Mr. Watkins. "But I just feel more comfortable talking with white servers. By the way, I don't want to have Peter either. He spilled the coffee twice already on my laptop."

At this point another line rang, and according to the Royal Hotel's high standards Johnny placed Mr. Watkins on hold.

Mr. Watkins was a top VIP at the Royal. He had already spent thousands of dollars at the hotel and recently booked a major conference for next year.

Most servers were busy delivering orders, and only Louis, an African American employee, was present, waiting for the next order. Johnny also noticed Mary as she was walking back from the cafeteria.

1. Should Johnny accommodate Mr. Watkins's first request?

2. How about Peter?

3. Assume that Mr. Watkins requests a male therapist in the Royal Spa? Would you accommodate that request?

Notes and Responses to Case Questions:

Case 69

The Cake Order

Case Type:	Incident Case
Main Subject:	Harassment
Who's Who:	• Rusty Fitzgerald, *Pastry Chef*
	• Lucy Moores, *Rusty's Friend*

Rusty, the pastry chef, was exhausted. She had been without an assistant pastry chef for four months and still there were no potential candidates to interview. "Let's see what's going on next week," she said to herself.

The Royal Hotel will be hosting a major VIP conference for CruiseDream, an International Cruise Line company. On Friday evening, a dinner dance will conclude the event. "The usual stuff," she thought. The company requested a huge strawberry shortcake with custom decoration. According to the banquet event order, the details of the cake design will be directly e-mailed to pastry. When she opened the e-mail, she could not believe her eyes. The attached photo showed a bare-breasted mermaid, but sculpted with unrealistic-sized breasts. Rusty was shocked and opened her drawer containing training documents and handouts she received at orientation. She remembered that the Royal Hotel is pledged to create a "harassment-free" environment and that the hotel protects its employees from harassment caused by nonemployees. Then she called Lucy, her best friend, who worked at a local law firm as a secretary. She could not understand all the words Lucy used but later remembered one term: *hostile environment*.

The next day, she filed a complaint at the State Commission Against Discrimination.

1. Hospitality organizations in general are especially vulnerable to incidents of sexual harassing behaviors. Why?

2. A hostile environment is created when sexual behaviors have the purpose or effect of unreasonably interfering with an individual's work performance or

creating an intimidating, hostile, or offensive work environment. From the information presented in this case, can this situation be considered harassment? Why or why not?

3. What steps can an employer take to avoid potential liability?

Notes and Responses to Case Questions:

I Am Not Your Slave!

Case Type:	Head Case
Main Subjects:	Diversity, Feedback, Harassment, Respect, Stereotypes
Who's Who:	• John Jones, *Restaurant Assistant Manager*
	• Ben Cotten, *Server Assistant* Ben Cotten, *Restaurant Server*

I t was a rainy and chilly night, and most guests at the Royal Hotel decided to stay in and have dinner at the hotel restaurant. John, the assistant manager, was in charge of the restaurant tonight. They were completely booked. To make matters worse, at 5 P.M. the food runner called in sick.

Instead of assigning someone to run the food, they agreed during the pre-meal meeting that everyone will run his or her own food and that the chef will page John if there is a problem.

John did his best. He was everywhere to ensure that the restaurant ran smoothly. The pager went off at 7 P.M. The chef was nervous because the food plated for two large tables was sitting on the kitchen counter. John looked around and Ben, one of the server assistants, seemed to be available. "Ben! Come! Let's run the food!" shouted John.

Ben came over and said, "You know, John, I am not your slave! No one should speak to us like that! By the way, I am busy with bread service," said Ben as he left.

John finally found another server to run the food and was wondering what he did wrong. "Is it something to do with that fact the Ben is African American and I am white?"

1. What are the typical stereotypes about African Americans?
2. What are the key values that are associated with the African American community? What major issues are important to African Americans?
3. John is clearly caught in a difficult situation. Where should he begin?
4. What would you suggest to happen when they meet to discuss the issue?
5. When speaking with an employee, how can we ensure that everyone feels a sense of equality?

Notes and Responses to Case Questions:

Image © J. Helgason, 2009. Used under license from Shutterstock.com

Name Calling

Case Type:	**Incident Case**
Main Subjects:	**Diversity, Harassment**
Who's Who:	• Lori Canelle, *Spa Manager*
	• Mahmoud Hassani, *Spa Employee*
	• Caitlin Smith, *Hotel Guest*

"Hey Mike, how are you?" asked Lori, the Spa manager.

"I am doing fine, but you know, my name is not Mike. I am Mahmoud, and I would really like to be called by my name," replied Mahmoud.

"I know …" Lori said, smiling. "I just have a hard time pronouncing your name. Also think about our clientele. Using a name like Mike will increase your chance to be noticed and be recommended as employee of the month. Anyway, did you offer a drink to Mrs. Smith? She just finished her aerobics class," said Lori.

1. Would you consider calling the employee Mike racially derogatory?

2. From the information presented in this case, can this situation be considered harassment? Why or why not?

3. What can the Royal Hotel do to minimize the possibility of this type of harassment?

Notes and Responses to Case Questions:

Image © Dmitriy Shironosov, 2009. Used under license from Shutterstock.com

A Strong Accent

Case Type:	Issue Case
Main Subjects:	Coaching, Discrimination, Diversity, Promotion
Who's Who:	• Carlos Diaz, *Guest Services Manager*
	• Attila Kuncze, *Houseman*

Attila was knocking on the door of Carlos, the Guest Services manager's office.

"How is everything in Housekeeping, Attila?" asked Carlos.

"Good! I heard that you are looking for a concierge. I am really interested in this position," replied Attila.

"Honestly, I think your verbal communication skills would hinder your ability to perform well behind the Concierge desk," answered Carlos.

"I know I have an accent, but I haven't had any problems in the past," said the Hungarian Attila.

"You may not realize it but you are extremely difficult to understand," pointed out Carlos.

"Have customers complained about my accent?" asked Attila.

"Your heavy accent would make it a little difficult for our English-speaking customers to understand. I really think you should take an English course and work on your enunciation," said Carlos. This concluded the discussion.

1. Can you refuse a job or promotion to someone who doesn't speak English well enough to do the job properly?

2. What advice might you have for the hotel?

Notes and Responses to Case Questions:

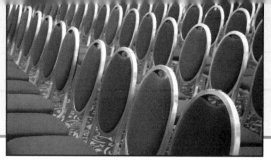

Case 73

The Empty Conference Room

Case Type:	Issue Case
Main Subjects:	Diversity, Religion
Who's Who:	• Rhiannon Palmer, *Convention Services Manager*
	• Fred Poitier, *Banquet Server*

Phone Call

"Good afternoon, Convention Services. Rhiannon speaking. How may I assist you?"

"Hi Rhiannon. This is Fred, the banquet server."

"What can I do for you Fred?" asked Rhiannon.

"We have received the event schedule for next month and I see that the second week is rather slow," answered Fred.

"Yes, that's right," answered Rhiannon.

"I am wondering if we could use one of the conference rooms to hold a prayer group. Six of us in Banquets belong to the same church. Of course, we would pay all the costs," added Fred.

"Carpet cleaning is scheduled for that week," replied Rhiannon hesitantly. "Can I call you back?" she asked, ending the conversation.

1. How would you advise Rhiannon? Should the hotel allow this conference room usage?

2. During lunch break, Fred engages another employee in a polite discussion of why his faith should be embraced. The other employee disagrees with Fred's exhortation, but does not ask that the conversation stop. Should the Royal Hotel restrict such speech?

Notes and Responses to Case Questions:

Case 74

Special Skills

Case Type:	Incident Case
Main Subjects:	Discipline, Diversity, Insubordination, Job Design/Job Description
Who's Who:	• Luis Vargas, *PBX Operator*
	• Kalinda Stenton, *PBX Manager*

"Luis, could you please do me a favor?" asked Kalinda, the PBX manager.

"Sure, what is that?" smiled Luis.

"There is a guest from Mexico in the business center who needs someone to translate some brief documents. He doesn't understand English at all. He's waiting for you. No worries, I'll cover you!"

"I'm not sure Kalinda," replied Luis. "I was born in Colombia and I came here at the age of 4. When my friends talked to me in Spanish, I replied to them in English. My parents chose to raise me in an English-only household. I made efforts to learn Spanish through classes in middle school but *my* vocabulary is really limited."

"*Your Spanish* is obviously way *better than mine*. We can only achieve our goals if we work as a team," Kalinda insisted.

"I prefer focusing on my own duties," Luis answered. "I don't feel comfortable about this assignment. I'm a switchboard operator, and being an interpreter or translator is not included in my job description."

"Do you realize that the failure to follow reasonable and lawful instructions is considered insubordination?" Kalinda said angrily. "Please go home. You're suspended for two days!"

1. Is disciplinary action warranted? Why or why not?

2. How could problems of this nature be avoided in the future?

Reference

The case is inspired by a situation described in:

Alexander Hamilton Institute. (2000). *The Employee Problem Solver* (Accent discrimination, pp. 1–9). Ramsey, NJ: Alexander Hamilton Institute.

Notes and Responses to Case Questions:

The Bamboo Ceiling

Case Type:	**Issue Case**
Main Subjects:	**Discrimination, Diversity, Stereotypes**
Who's Who:	• Charlie Jones, *Director of Engineering*
	• Robert Kunz, *General Manager*
	• William Ming, *IT Manager*
	• Katherine Norton, *Director of Human Resources*
	• Louise Rausch, *Director of Finance*
	• Yan Yao, *Assistant Director of Finance*

"We need to provide a continuous flow of talented candidates to meet the Royal's management needs. The executive committees' role is to identify high-potential employees, capable of rapid advancement to positions of higher responsibilities," Robert Kunz reminded everybody after the lunch break at the yearly succession planning meeting. "Who is next?" he asked.

"Yuan, from Finance," Katherine, the Human Resource director helped him out.

"How is he doing?" asked Robert as he turned to the others.

"He has been tracking our expenses in an organized manner, and as you know he was instrumental in guiding William in the implementation of our new computer system. You know, they are great at crunching numbers!" said Louise, his boss.

"Yuan is always so polite, and patient with me. It's a pleasure doing business with him," smiled Charlie, from Engineering. "It's good to have people like Yuan in Finance."

"Okay, let's move on," Robert said.

1. What are the typical stereotypes about Asian Americans?

2. How can positive stereotypes negatively affect Asian Americans' upward mobility?

3. How can organizations help Asian Americans to overcome cultural traits that are more pronounced within the Asian community?

Notes and Responses to Case Questions:

Additional Notes